Get up, Create, Break out

Practical faith-inspired wisdom for women who want to re-launch their careers after a break

Veronica Anthony

Get up, Create, Break out

Onwards and Upwards Publishers
Berkeley House, 11 Nightingale Crescent, Leatherhead,
Surrey, KT24 6PD.
www.onwardsandupwards.org

Printed in the UK.

ISBN: 978-1-907509-82-7
Typeface: Sabon LT
Graphic design: Leah-Maarit

The author will donate royalties from the sale of this book to
Smart Opportunities for Women

Testimonials

"An inspiring book, just like its author. Thank you, Veronica, for playing a big part in inspiring me to keep going and believing in myself. I thank you from the bottom of my heart!"

K.W.

Re-launched her career after a ten-year break

"Before getting some support from Veronica, I felt really discouraged and frustrated. I now feel confident and have a clear job search strategy. The great news is I have an interview next week. Simply amazing!"

E.S.

Re-launched her career after a five-year break

"Veronica understands the challenges that women face. She has given me useful advice as well as the confidence to achieve my career-change goals."

J.A.

Re-launched her career after a seven-year break

"I could not have gotten this job without your support. You are doing a great job. Thank you Veronica."

C.P.

Re-launched her career after a nine-year break

"Veronica is always attentive to the needs of everyone within her sphere of work and recognises where inequalities may hamper individuals development. She always brings her coaching and business skills to help others overcome barriers to employment and future pathways and career development."

C.S. & M.O.

Training providers

"Thanks for helping me to fully understand my skills and capabilities. I now feel so confident about managing my career."

T.A.

Got a great job after university

Acknowledgements

To all the wonderful women who have allowed me to be
a part of their re-launch journey:

*I have learnt to see the world through your eyes,
and my life can never remain the same.*

To the women who have shared their stories in this book:

Thanks for your desire to make a difference. I feel humbled.

To my parents, Abel and Victoria:

*Thanks for putting up with me all these years.
I can never repay you for all you have done for me.*

To Andrew, Victoria, Mabel, Marian and Margaret:

*I am blessed to be surrounded by so much love and support.
I love you guys.*

To pastors Rod and Julie Anderson:

*I am amazed by your humility, gentle leadership and passion to make
Jesus known. The world needs more leaders like you.*

To Carol Sinker:

*Thanks for believing in me; your unwavering confidence in me
has made me soar like an eagle.*

To Olufunmilayo, my precious friend and prayer buddy:

*I want you to know that your constant encouragement has been
invaluable to me on this journey called life.
I value your friendship, girl.*

Acknowledgements

To Suzy, Karis and Uche:

Thanks for showing me what a courageous spirit looks like. Don't stop living boldly.

To David Bays, Claudine Reid and Mike Ferrera:

You have helped me find my voice. You have challenged me to break out into God's purpose for me.

To pastors Bennett and Debbie:

Thanks for showing me the truth in God's Word when I was hurting and couldn't see clearly.

To Paul Barron and the Kent Foundation crew:

Thanks for believing in this 'mum-preneur'.

To Carmel Millar, Tim Cowley and Andrea Harrison:

I find your leadership and management styles refreshing. I have learnt so much from you in such a short time.

Finally, to the team at Onwards and Upwards Publishers:

Thanks for believing in the message of this book. As a result of this partnership, many women will be challenged to step into God's plan for them. I have enjoyed working with you.

To my home team.

Tony, my husband and best friend: I bless God for that day many moons ago when our paths crossed. Ours is a story of persistence, love, courage and hope. I securely journey along with you because God leads the way.

Joshua and Virtue: you can never understand the impact which your four-word song ("You can do it") has had on my life. It is such an honour and privilege to be your mother.

And with all my heart, I dedicate this book to my wonderful Saviour, Jesus Christ. Forever I am changed by your love and compassion. I really don't know why you love me so much!

Contents

About the Author 8

Foreword by Julie Anderson 9

Introduction 11

GET UP 15

1. I am a Professional Woman; Get Me out of Here! 17

2. Taking the First Step 22

3. Diamonds in the Mud 26

4. Through God's Eyes 42

CREATE 53

5. Ideas Don't Stay Hot Forever 55

6. What do You Want? 61

7. The Journey of Discovery 68

8. Which Way? 75

9. What is in Your Hand? 79

BREAK OUT 107

10. Moving Mountains 109

11. Let Your Light Shine 129

12. Lessons by Doing 135

Reflective Exercises for Part I: Get Up 146

Reflective Exercises for Part II: Create 155

Reflective Exercises for Part III: Break Out....................162

A Quick 'How To' Guide for your Re-launch Action Plan........164

Epilogue: Still Walking on Water 170

Useful Websites and Organisations 172

Connect..180

About the Author

Many women have been inspired and supported to re-launch their careers by Veronica Anthony's teaching and coaching. As well as being a Career Development Consultant, Veronica speaks at conferences and events, and supports the business performance of public sector organisations as an Organisational Development Specialist.

She runs the *Get up, Create, Breakout* programme and is the founder of Smart Opportunities for Women – a social enterprise dedicated to helping disadvantaged women access, create and maximise opportunities. She and her husband, Tony, are blessed with two children.

Foreword by Julie Anderson

Veronica Anthony is a superb encourager. When the draft of this book was sent to me I felt touched by the passion in Veronica's heart that comes through in her writing. I feel honoured that she invited me to write the foreword for her timely message.

We live in an era when it's more vital than ever, as women, that we train our spirit and live from the place of confidence knowing what God has said in His covenant Word to us, as well as in the gentle beauty and the fear of the Lord. In order to fulfil our chosen places in what we work at each day, we need to pray to see our careers become successful and produce the heavenly abundance intended. As women we must rise up and move out in life, and live from our place of passion. Veronica's book offers amazing practical 'how-to's to help you live your dream.

One of the charities I founded and lead is the Deborah Company UK, which gathers women who are modern day biblical Deborahs. By that I mean women who make the effort to 'rise up' out of their situations, sometimes often really difficult ones, whether within their own homes and families, or outside at work, in business, or in their churches; women who rise up both within and outside the marketplace, who face many challenges but understand their true identity in God and live from the security of having no need to compete – with nothing to protect or prove. Even in gender issues, working with other successful men or women, women who rise up secure in God are being mightily used by Him. Women who rise up are changing our societies.

The message in her book of the unconditional love of God for both men and women, and the revelation of just how much God cares so greatly about what we do and how we live, is very clear. I agree with her line of thought that God blesses us with various talents and gifts and cares about what we do with them, and that while He wants us to be successful, He is more interested in our character development. I have personally come across many situations in which a woman's hateful attitude and a man's hateful attitude converge in a clash of strife.

Veronica's story has many helpful insights in how to overcome obstacles to success and how to get up out of a pit, or a tight corner, and move into a place where creativity begins to flow and you see the future from God's perspective and live 'in the now' peacefully. This book will inspire anyone who reads it to break out of their mundane into the miraculous flow of destiny. When your journey through life turns onto the path upon which you understand how to move mountains and shine by 'who you are' and 'what you do', you have then discovered the right path for your life and find you have every resource already in your hand to begin your life assignment.

My core value is 'honouring heaven', and I live with a passion each day towards that end. My experience of working in the corporate world, along with my academic qualifications, achievements, skills and capabilities, helps me fulfil my task of living this daily. In all my relationships I make the effort each morning to take time to seek God and His way of doing things, and I meditate and pray over each day. I believe we are all *chosen* by God for specific assignments and tasks, and yet He has gifted us for our own particular path – which all works together for good, fitting into a divine master plan. I believe God's mercies are fresh (Lamentations 3:23), and as I seek wisdom and apply it to my everyday situations, I believe God wants us to live in high spirit and help others bring in victorious strategies for their own personal lives.

It is time for skilful, renewed minds to rule wisely. As Christian women we must learn to reign and release the authority of heaven, with sweet dominion, in cascades of victory falling down into the earth around us. Women who determine to rise up are changing nations.

This book is a must read if you are carrying an unborn dream to fulfil your career as well as your calling as a wife, mother, leader, influencer, nation changer. It reveals many rich nuggets of practical action that can help you step forward.

Julie Anderson
Founder, The Deborah Company UK & The Prayer Foundation
Senior Leader, Commonwealth Church

Introduction

From passion to compassion

God loves women. He blesses us with various talents and gifts, and cares about what we do with them. While He wants us to be successful, He is more interested in our character. When I initially started supporting women back into work, I was filled with so much passion but had the wrong attitude and a twisted understanding of the word 'success'. Growing up, I saw a lot of gender oppression around me which made me resolve to be a successful woman and help others become successful too. The only problem was I had a lot of pain and anger buried beneath. I was angry with the world's system, and although I would never admit it, I was angry with men and God too.

I was on a mission to empower women and show them how to create opportunities. I started running community workshops and coaching women. Soon I was developing and delivering various training programmes supporting both highly skilled and low-skilled men and women. Through a divine arrangement, I started delivering government programmes focused on helping people back into work. One of these programmes is targeted at lone parents; on average about 98% of participants are women. Through the pain and struggles of many of these women, God began to work on my heart, and moved me from passion to compassion. He started giving me visions and dreams about women and began to teach me the truth in His word, showing me how this truth can set women free and cause them to flourish both inside and outside the marketplace. I remember once, after reflecting on all the struggles that many women face, I asked God a direct question, and all He whispered into my heart was, "Tell them I love them."

God's love means many things and covers all areas, one of which is 'what we do with our lives'. This is where our careers come in. For me, the word 'career' means 'a chosen pursuit undertaken for a significant period of a person's life'. This could mean setting up a business, working for an employer, running a charity, working from

11

home, helping out in the church or community whilst being a stay-at-home mum, and more.

You may be feeling rejected and despondent after several attempts to re-launch your career without much success. Or you may feel as though all you've done is 'have kids' and nothing else. I want you to know that motherhood is the most important job in the world. God designed and equipped women especially to look after His children and build the next generation. You are precious to Him and He sees you differently. His definition of success is different to ours; this is why making peace with God and your situation, and cultivating a heart of gratitude, is the best place to start from.

Everyone wants to hear that re-launching one's career after a career break (or period of no employment) is quick and easy. Just follow steps 1 to 5 and – *poof* – you're there! Sadly that's not the case. All kinds of resistance, emotions, and unexpected issues will crop up. They sure did for me and many of the women I have worked with. And there will be times when you will want to quit, times when you wonder why you're even bothering.

Sometimes we are faced with huge mountains that threaten to prevent us from achieving our goals. There will be times when you'll feel really down – times when money is so tight and letters of unsuccessful applications flood your email inbox. People may tell you that you can't do it or try to influence you to settle for less. You may question whether there's anything out there for you. It's in times like this that your husband's snoring sounds like crashing thunder, the children's screams threaten to burst your ear drums, and your friends all seem busy and successful... Nothing seems to be going right, and you want to give up and run away.

Psalm 56:3
When I am afraid, I put my trust in you.

Proverbs 3:5
Trust in the Lord with all your heart and lean not on your own understanding...

I wrote this book with you in mind, and I encourage you not to give up but to take action starting from today. That action may mean taking a step back and giving yourself room to reflect, to refresh, to regroup and of course to re-launch. I cannot overemphasise the importance of taking time out to really reflect on who you are: your journey, attitude, motivation, desires, etc.

This is a great place to start from. Think of this book as a useful referencing tool as you journey on.

I am rooting for you!

Veronica Anthony

Get up, Create, Break out

Get Up

If you don't get up,
you will stay down.

"Shake off your dust, rise up, sit enthroned, O
Jerusalem. Free yourself from the chains on your neck,
O captive Daughter of Zion."

Isaiah 52:2

Get up, Create, Break out

CHAPTER ONE

I am a Professional Woman; Get Me out of Here!

The year was 2008 and I was on maternity leave following the birth of my first child. I could hear the sound of the night. At last I had some peace and quiet…

No, don't envy me just yet. I've got books scattered all around me. My hair looks like it hasn't been kissed by a comb in ages. With a cup of hot water and my laptop as companions, I am determined to make some headway with this research. I have become tired of doing nothing about the business idea that has lied dormant in my head. With eight weeks of maternity leave left before returning to work, I know it will be almost impossible to focus solely on the research once the 'nine to five' race set in again. So I have made up my mind to commit a few night hours a week to researching my idea

It's 1:04 am. My head feels very heavy. This is due largely to the flu that invaded my body a couple of days ago. My body's telling me it needs some sleep, but I decide not to respond. I know that time is a very precious commodity in my world right now. My day is fully packed with looking after my six-month-old son and ensuring that everything runs well in our home. When I am not changing dirty nappies, I'm cooking, cleaning, washing or… The list goes on.

Where's Mum when I need her? Well, Mum lives many miles away in another country with my dad, and although she visited and stayed for a month when I had my son, her visit ended too soon. My husband helps as much as he can when he is at home, but his daily work routine means he is out of the house from 7 am to 7 pm. His gentle snoring breaks through the quiet night and creates a rhythm with the jazz music playing in the background. This night is definitely no night of passion, so unfortunately there will be no exploration of beautifully crafted bodies...

The days flew by in quick succession, and soon it was time to return to work. I was looking forward to maintaining a professional image and spending time with adults again. I had grown tired of staying at home every single day. The occasional visits to the hospital and sure start group activities didn't really count for much. Having suffered from mild depression, I couldn't wait to rejuvenate my senses. I enjoyed the time I spent at home bonding with my son, but I knew deep in my heart that I wasn't cut out to be a full time stay-at-home mum, and many times I came close to shouting these words: "Please, get me out of here!"

Soon it was time to resume work, and like I had imagined, there was nothing exciting. I soon slipped into my old way of life, the only difference being that I was now a mother with breasts fully laden with lactose milk.

The great thing about returning to work was that my manager enhanced my motivation and made me feel valued by allowing me to work from home one day a week. We found a good nursery close to the house, which made it easy for my husband and me to drop off and pick up our son. I carried his picture everywhere and would often look at his picture while at work and tell him how much I loved him. This helped subdue the pangs of guilt that often threatened to shatter my inner world. And the good old breast pads came in handy when I decided to stop breastfeeding. After a couple of months, I had become a 'working mum' expert.

Or so I thought...

2009-2010 – The boat is rocked

"Happy birthday!"

It was my son's first birthday party. The day started really well; there was so much food, lots of music, lovely presents, and the birthday boy was really excited. I was enjoying my role as the hostess and mother of the celebrant until...

"Oh! You didn't tell us you were expecting another one so soon!"

I almost fainted when a woman uttered these words. I gave her a look that would have made a dead man shiver in his grave, but this had no effect whatsoever as she repeated her statement with confidence and a mischievous twinkle in her eye. I mumbled a quick reply, tried to remain civil and hurriedly moved on to exchange pleasantries with another guest.

By the time another guest made a similar statement, I had started to panic. Could this be true? But how? Don't contraceptives work anymore?

The result of the pregnancy test confirmed my fears. I *was* pregnant! I could not believe it. I didn't feel ready and it was tough listening to people's comments. My parents did not help matters when they commented that my husband and I should have taken precautions. I knew they were concerned, especially as I had had some health complications with my first pregnancy. I just didn't need all the barrage of questions and comments.

I didn't know how to tell them at work, but I didn't have to worry for too long as the members of my six-woman team found out sooner than I expected.

Then, the comments started.

"Oh, you smart thing, you'll soon be off again. Are you sure you'll come back this time?"

"You are so wise to have them close to each other."

"Aren't you too young to have two of them so close together? I had mine in my late thirties, you know…"

I had to endure months of irritating and annoying comments. It didn't help that I was feeling constantly tired and had a lot of pain in my pelvic area. It was all too much for me so I decided to start my maternity leave eight weeks before my due date. Can you really blame me?

Late 2010 – Back at work

I think the whole process of going through labour and bringing forth another new life had changed something in me; I felt more purposeful and driven to take control of my future. I was more determined than ever to harness my skills and make a real difference at work. I was on cloud nine.

I got a rude shock on my first day back at work. Having had no 'keep-in-touch' meetings, I was not prepared for the major changes that had taken place.

Everything had changed. My team had merged with other sub-teams and was now part of a larger corporate team. Only one member of my old team remained. Others had either taken the voluntary redundancy package or left. Alarm bells started to ring, but I decided not to be bothered. And even when the rumours of bad practice by senior management filtered into my ears, I made up my mind not to get infected. But how long could I stay immune?

January 2011 – Time to re-launch

Things quickly deteriorated but I kept on 'psyching' myself. The final straw that 'broke the camel's back' was the downgrading of my responsibilities and the constant bullying by my line manager. It was almost as if it was a crime to have been away from the organisation for a while. Life at work was stressful and demotivating. Being part of a team where, amongst many other things, senior management didn't fully comprehend and embrace the concept and benefits of flexible working made life a complete nightmare. I felt I had to choose between 'going to work' and 'staying at home'. I wanted to utilise my skills and did not want to give up working. All I wanted was a flexible solution.

I knew I had more to give and that any extra time spent working in such an environment would destroy my confidence. How could I settle for less? But then there was the issue of money. How would we cope as a young family with a mortgage and no real savings? Thinking of the uncertainty made me really anxious. Eventually, I decided to take some time to reflect on what I had going for me: my core values, passion, professional experience, academic qualifications, achievements, commercial exposure, skills, capabilities etc. I took out more time to meditate and pray, and then wrote out my different options, highlighting pros and cons for each alternative.

Only then was I able to make a much needed decision. Yes, you guessed right! I handed in my resignation letter and decided I was going to launch out on my own – something I should've done much earlier.

Walking on water

Following my resignation, my husband and I were under a lot of financial pressure, and there were days when we had almost nothing to eat. I must confess that it was during this period that I began to really understand what it means to trust God day by day. We experienced miracles, from surprise cash gifts to having money returned to us unexpectedly. There were times when I was filled with doubts and came close to giving up, especially when there was no work coming through.

Late 2011, in particular, was a really tough period, but just as I was about to give up, God opened doors of opportunity and I have not looked back since. I began to understand that God expects me to play my part with humility, trust and total acknowledgement that He has my best interests at heart. It was amazing to see God intervening on my behalf when I took simple steps of faith through the tools and seeds that I placed in His hands.

Questions for reflection

What is your present situation?

_____

_____

_____

_____

How do you feel about your present situation?

_____

_____

_____

_____

CHAPTER TWO

Taking the First Step

In 2011, six months after returning to work following the birth of my daughter, the work environment was incredibly toxic and all I could think of was getting out at all costs. My confidence had taken a serious dive, and I constantly felt miserable. There were lots of sleepless or broken nights. I really have no idea how my husband put up with me at this time.

Prior to this, the Holy Spirit had told me that 2011 would be a year to 'walk on water'. I had always felt it strongly that I would run my own business, so based on this I was quick to jump to the conclusion that the ill-treatment I was receiving was an indirect push from God to leave my job. Looking back now, I left with the wrong attitude, filled with pride and anger. I felt I was too good for such an organisation. I was angry with the consultant for bullying me, and the head of the team for allowing such bad practice.

The stepping stone

The first few weeks following my resignation were not so bad because I jumped straight into doing some freelance work for a training provider. Out of the blue, I received a call from the managing director of a training company. At that time, I did not know this woman personally, but when I was with a previous employer I had commissioned her organisation to deliver some in-house training. She explained that her organisation had won some career development and outplacement contracts, and wanted to know if I would be happy to lead this arm of the business and develop all necessary training materials on an associate basis. This opportunity could not have come at a better time; I was thrilled and agreed.

When I got off the phone after speaking to the managing director, I became petrified and started imagining things going wrong. What if I would 'mess up'? What if the materials I would produce would be substandard? How could this woman believe so much in me? And then my thoughts went into defeat mode. I felt I was not good enough for this opportunity. I started reflecting on the fact that I was black and young and so would not be accepted by all-white and/or older audiences. For days my thoughts threatened to drown me. I remember telling my husband over and over that I did not think I was good enough. I am sure he must have gotten fed up of me constantly putting myself down, but he kept on encouraging and reminding me of my previous achievements.

None of the things I had feared happened. On the contrary, I received very good feedback from participants (98% of whom were white and older) from various organisations. I was initially contracted to deliver outplacement solutions for one public sector organisation, but with increased funding cuts and reorganisations, this led to more and more work with other public sector organisations. It was a dream come true.

Hitting rock bottom

As is the norm in the world of training, where a course or programme may be in vogue today and gone the next day, the demand for outplacement solutions reduced drastically, particularly because many organisations had finished their restructuring. This meant I had little or no work. For the first time in my life, I was technically unemployed. I must confess that it was an incredibly scary period for me. My husband was also facing challenges at work, and in fact there was a time when we were both at home without jobs to go to. My confidence took a further knock, and all the anger I had bottled up against the consultant who had ill-treated me resurfaced. I started blaming her for making me resign from my job when I did. I could no longer remember the recent success I had just had, developing and delivering outplacement solutions to over four hundred employees and senior managers from different organisations. Everything that could go wrong started going wrong. For the first time in my life I began to rely on overdrafts. Letters of late payments flooded our inbox – and then the panic attacks started. Twice ambulance men visited our home because my husband thought I was having a heart attack. It was as if I was having a terrible nightmare.

I actually had an idea of what I wanted to do but was not quite sure how or where to start from because I was so overwhelmed by all that was happening to me. I could not even function well in my roles as a wife and mum. Sex became a chore and life got really boring. Now I understand that God sometimes allows us to go through certain experiences to refine us and prepare us for the next phase of our life. During this time, I reached rock bottom, and for the first time I understood what it meant to have God as my only rock. I started to seek God's face; it initially started with me crying out to God, then I would get a nudge to read a scripture or watch a programme on one of the Christian TV stations.

Reaching out

I felt incredibly lonely and realised I wanted more of God. I couldn't do this on my own so I started searching for a women's group where I could hear the truth of God's Word, pray with others, share my experience and learn from the experience of other women. Unfortunately, I could not find any relevant group to join, close to where we lived. So I decided to start a prayer group with a few women that I knew. I sent a text message to a couple of women, and soon we started meeting together to pray every first Thursday of the month from 10 am to 1 pm, which worked really well with school drop off and pick up times. I found myself looking forward to the meetings and my faith was strengthened.

A change of heart

God started working on my heart. It was at this time that I learnt the importance of forgiveness. I started making peace with God and my situation. It wasn't until I made peace with my situation, by accepting it as God's starting point for me, that things began to slowly fall in place.

I don't know what your exact circumstances are. You may be a stay-at-home mum with grown up kids and an unsupportive husband, looking to re-launch your career. You may be a mum with young kids keen to use your skills in the workplace or community. Or you may have recently been made redundant and are feeling defeated and bitter. I encourage you to speak peace over your situation and thank God for all He has done and for the new opportunities awaiting you. Take a positive posture and choose faith instead of fear and anxiety. If, like me, you've been proud or resentful, ask God for forgiveness and then get ready for an adventure.

Questions for reflection

What do you need to repent of?

\
\
\

What are you holding on to, that you need to let go of?

\
\
\

Who do you need to forgive?

\
\
\

CHAPTER THREE

Diamonds in the Mud

Diamonds in their true form shine beautifully and reflect the light that is around them. Now, picture diamonds in layers of mud that have been accumulated over time. The mud not only reduces the amount of light that the diamonds can reflect, in most cases it prevents the diamonds from being seen at all. And if the diamonds cannot be seen, their true worth and value cannot be appreciated or communicated to someone else.

For the major part of my life, I felt I wasn't good enough. I actually believed I was unattractive and didn't have well-endowed body proportions. So strong were my beliefs about myself that I would roll pieces of cloth and insert them into my bra just to make my breasts look bigger. There are so many tales I can share with you, but I am sure you get the picture. I grew up thinking and feeling I wasn't pretty enough, stylish enough, attractive enough... I had a middle name and it was 'Insecurity'. When you don't feel like you are good enough, the enemy will capitalise on this and make you believe that you don't deserve good things or that you cannot achieve certain things.

The majority of the women that I have met and interacted with (who have been away from the workplace for a while, or who have never worked, or who are thinking of starting a career in a new sector) often find the idea of re-launching pretty daunting. Like diamonds in the mud, layers of low self-esteem, loneliness, insecurities, financial pressures, inadequate or lack of spousal support, different forms of abuse etc., accumulate around these women and slowly chip away at their confidence until they forget about their real worth and/or underestimate what they are capable of doing and achieving.

Beulah's story

Beulah works in a Business Support role and re-launched her career after a five-year break.

It was always my heart's desire to take time off work when my children came along. My desire was to be with them for the first five years of their lives. This was important to me and so, when my first child came along, I did not debate it. I really did not think as far as the second child, but when she came along as well, I knew that I wanted the same for her. However, I went back to work on a part-time basis just before my first turned five.

Although not my perfect plan, as I would have been happier to stay at home with my children until they were five and look after the wellbeing of my family, I was happy to go back to work. Working part-time meant that I was still able to spend time with my younger one and even pick the older one up from school occasionally.

My main reason for going back to work was to regain my independence as I was not getting the necessary support from my husband; I felt limited and was unable to do so many things for the children and myself. I also wanted to prove to him that I could 'be somebody' too. The truth is, only one of the reasons was worthwhile (going back to regain my independence and confidence). I have since learnt that rather than trying to prove things to others, I need to simply focus on being whom God has created me to be. His approval is the only thing that counts.

In going back to work, my greatest challenge was overcoming my low self-esteem and believing in myself. I did not believe that someone could need what I had – my experiences, my skills, my personality, my qualifications, my knowledge, etc. Another challenge that I faced was more practical – getting help, advice and support in putting a current and workable CV together and applying for jobs.

I am lucky to have a friend who specialises in career development. To me she is more than a friend. Amongst other things, she is also my 'whip' and she definitely inspired me to believe that I could go back to work! I believe that anyone that has had a career break, particularly under challenging circumstances, needs someone that can take them under their wings and show them how to fly again.

When God has a plan and purpose for one's life, sometimes one begins to take the path without fully realising what is driving one.

I went back to work with children. The interesting thing that I discovered was that I had worked with children most of my life without realising it. The jobs I had taken on in the past had always included some aspect of children and/or their safety and development.

I saw going back to work as a bridging gap – as I would have taken any job when that particular job came along. I so wanted to gain some independence and confidence. However, starting the job also gave me the opportunity to re-think the possibilities in my career aspiration. I would say that I have not fully re-launched my career as I do not believe that I am where I want to be yet. However, getting that first job after five years gave me the confidence to get back on track and pursue afresh the career that I had started out to build in the first place.

For me, there are still challenges. I have to keep believing that despite the competition out there, I can do it. I have to believe that despite all the negative things that have been said against what I want to achieve, I can do it. I have to believe that I know what I am doing. I have to believe that I too can attract someone's attention with my application form or CV. It is still a challenge, and I often get my good friend to check my work for me. For this reason, it is important to have continued support. It takes time and real dedication to succeed. Above all, I have to believe that I can do anything through God who strengthens me.

Although it may sound like a cliché, I now believe, more than I did before, that I too am worthy to apply for a good job. This was made possible by God through my friend. When you are feeling low I believe that you need someone who can get you up and point you in the right direction, someone to help you refocus on your vision. But more than anything else, I believe you need unwavering faith.

Dropping the baggage

Over the years, I have accumulated many memories, some of which I want to cherish for a lifetime and others which I just want to forget. Unfortunately, I do not have a delete button to help delete my unpleasant or unwanted memories. Some of these memories were created when things did not go as I expected, when I failed at tasks and underachieved, and particularly when I was hurt by people close to me. For a greater part of my life, I held on to negative memories and felt I was not good enough. The tricky thing is that these feelings stayed with me as I grew up to become an adult and entered the workplace. I never actually realised how much baggage I was carrying despite the fact that these feelings kept popping up and trying to consume me.

You may be wondering how these things are connected to a career re-launch. If my own experience, and that of the people I have supported back to work, is anything to go by, I would say it has *everything* to do with it. In today's world it is hard to find someone without any emotional baggage. Maybe you were made redundant unfairly, your husband walked out on you, or perhaps you are in a loveless marriage where you've experienced a lot of verbal and emotional abuse. Many people have 'tapes' playing in their head as a result of the baggage they've carried for long. These head tapes rob them of their confidence and often threaten to stop, or succeed in preventing, them from taking action to re-launch their careers.

Do these tapes play in your head too?

- "I can't do it."
- "I have never been good at..."
- "He says I am not good enough, and I know he's probably right."
- "I am too old anyway; they'll probably go for a younger candidate."
- "I am not pretty."
- "Things never work for me."
- "Mum used to call me stupid; I guess I must be really stupid."
- "I always mess things up."
- "My bum is so flat."

- "No one would want to employ someone like me."
- "I look awful."

We do not have an inbuilt device to remove negative memories, but we can surely get rid of damages that these head tapes can do to us and take action to stop emotional baggage from holding us back.

Getting rid of my many bags

Everyone has their own way of dealing with their emotional baggage, and everyone takes their own time to come out of it. Here are some of the things that have helped me:

COUNSELLING

Over the years I built a shell around me which made it difficult for me to trust people or develop relationships with them. I had so much baggage in me. I knew I had a huge problem when I found it difficult to accept that my husband loved me. I recently had the privilege of being counselled by a man of God, during a time of adversity which shook my confidence. I thank God for the counselling and teaching I received from Pastor Bennett. At first I did not really know what to expect from the counselling sessions, and I wasn't sure they would have much of an impact. How wrong I was! Soon I began to dig through God's Word and started seeing myself through God's eyes. The Word of God came alive for me once again and slowly began to transform my life. I know that many people think counselling is a sign of weakness. On the contrary, it shows that you are strong enough to identify that you need help to overcome emotional baggage. I believe that the right type of counselling can be very helpful.

STUDYING, MEDITATING AND CONFESSING GOD'S WORD

I cannot tell you how much this helps me. Even now, when negative thoughts threaten to fill my mind, I release the Word of God. The Word of God for me is like a sharp arrow that counters and bursts the negative balloons of defeat, failure and rejection that sometimes try to overwhelm me. Reading and meditating on God's Word gives me a bank of positive promises to draw from when I feel low. God wants to take you on a 'truth journey' through studying His

Word. It will help you purge your negative thoughts and give you the ability to see the positives in your situation.

PRAYER

First of all, I want you to know that I struggled in the place of prayer for the major part of my life. For days I would carry on without praying and simply utter a few lines of prayer occasionally. I am still on my journey but thankfully things are different. I cannot overemphasise the power a woman will have if only she will pray. Prayer is one of the ways we release the will of God in our lives, and we must study the Word of God to know His will. God's will is that you are free from baggage and live a good life. As I began to study and pray God's Word, I slowly began to notice that my thoughts were becoming more positive and my attitude was generally getting better.

DELIVERANCE

Deliverance is being set free from spiritual bondages and barriers that hold us back from walking in victory. In their book, 'Pigs in the Parlor', Frank and Ida Hammond explain that deliverance is not a panacea or cure all, and admonish that every individual needs to find out what part deliverance can play and what benefits it offers. I know first-hand the benefits of deliverance; I struggled with some emotional problems and was constantly tormented by fear until I had the opportunity of being ministered to. As I am growing in my faith, I am learning how to listen to the Holy Spirit and use the authority I have as a child of God to sustain my deliverance and victories.

For some people, despite their best efforts to move forward in life, they are held down, not because they have not tried their best but because of deep, faulty, foundational issues that have not been dealt with. The Bible sums this up nicely:

Psalm 11:3
...if the foundations be destroyed, what can the righteous do?

Faulty foundations are established when individuals fail to adhere to the principles of God's Word as it relates to all areas of life – family, marriage, career, environment, etc. Many people are suffering for atrocities that were committed by their parents and ancestors such

31

as occultism, murder, sexual perversion, injustice, etc. I have only recently begun to look deeply into this area after asking God to reveal great and mighty secrets to me; since then I have been on a journey of discovery and learning which has led to liberation.

For those who believe that this applies to them, there are good books written by some Christian authors such as John Eckhardt and Apostle Onyechi Daniel that will equip you and show you how to deal with these issues. I have to stress that the death of Jesus and the blood He shed on the cross has already secured our deliverance. Our testimony is sure; we just need to believe and act on this.

LETTING GO

Although this was probably one of the most difficult things for me to do, when I made up my mind to forgive those who had hurt me or affected me negatively and let them go from my mind, I realised that I was really releasing *myself* from the toxic chain of bitterness and giving myself the licence to soar. Forgiveness is a key part of deliverance. Initially I thought it would be impossible to forgive; but that was because I was relying on my natural ability. Once I opened up my heart to receive God's grace, I found myself letting go.

POSITIVE REFLECTION

I notice that whenever I focus on previous achievements I get a faith boost. In trying times, this helps to turn my negative thoughts into positive thoughts. Being positive is powerful. And a big part of being positive is simply reminding yourself of your past successes.

When David faced the giant Goliath, he remembered the lion and the bear he had defeated in the past, and it gave him courage to go out and face Goliath. If you are going through a difficult time right now, let me remind you that this probably isn't the first challenge you've faced in your life. You've most likely overcome many challenges and learnt a lot of vital lessons. Like David, remember your past successes, then dig through the Word and get God's perspective.

SHARING WITH FRIENDS

I have a friend whom I confide in and pray with, and this has blessed me so much. Talking things over with her makes me feel better and lighter. However, there will always be some issues that will be inappropriate to discuss with friends. These are better left in God's hands.

How I have gained confidence

Confidence is an important ingredient for anyone who wants to re-launch successfully. If our confidence is low, we are far less likely to try or do something new. The good thing is that we can develop more confidence because no matter how much or how little we have we can always have more. It would be a lie to tell you that I am super-confident all of the time. Every now and again, I still find myself feeling low in confidence. The great thing is that when this happens, I know what to do to get myself back on track. Looking back, the following have been my main confidence-boosters:

READING THE BIBLE

Stories of heroes of faith such as Moses and the Red Sea, Joshua and the wall of Jericho, Daniel in the den of lions, Deborah, Esther, David and Goliath, Nehemiah, etc. strengthen me. Whenever I am working on a project that seems daunting, I take time to study the story of a Bible character who faced something similar. This builds my faith and helps me to take risks.

LEARNING FROM EAGLES

I was intrigued to learn that early in John Maxwell's career he contacted the top ten leaders in his field and offered them $100 to meet with him for thirty minutes so that he could ask them questions. Many granted his request and, fortunately for his thin wallet at that time, most declined to accept the $100. Some years ago, I decided to adopt this principle. Since then, I have made it a point of duty to contact successful leaders whom I admire and from whom I desire to learn. These people inspire me particularly because each one has overcome their own obstacles along the way. Sometimes, I would send an email or LinkedIn request for advice. Other times, I would request brief meetings to enable me ask questions and learn from them. Over two thirds of the leaders I have approached have responded positively. Listening to these leaders recounting their failures or some obstacles which they encountered on their way to success boosts my confidence and is a perfect reminder that 'everyone is human'. Over the years, I have also secured mentors through corporate and business mentoring schemes.

A NETWORK OF SUPPORT

I firmly believe that we all need people who believe in us and who are willing to give honest advice when required. I am lucky to have a few people around me who believe in me and constantly push me not to give up on my dreams. I probably wouldn't have written this book, but for the constant prodding of one of my sisters. I have been helped enormously by my mentors. Over time I gradually built up a group of fabulous mentors, people whom I respected with strengths in various areas, that I could have a chat with when I wasn't sure what to do in a certain situation. We all need great people like these around us. If you don't have a few mentors already, start thinking about who you know that you respect and admire, who might be able to give you their time. The amount of time may be as little as one hour per quarter.

To assess what type of support you have around you, a good place to start would be to define your relationships. Our relationships with people can influence us positively or negatively. Influence can be powerful and subtle, and so most times we don't know we are being influenced until it's a bit too late. Although peer pressure is commonly associated with young people, adults experience it as well. We need to assess our relationships and be careful whom we allow to influence us or our dreams.

RELATIONSHIP DEFINITION

If you are to achieve your goals, you will need to seriously assess your relationships. Doing this will help you to effectively manage them and identify those people that you need to limit your association with, expand your association with, or stop associating with.

I recommend that you get a notepad and start defining your existing relationships.

Let's take a look at some of the key people in your re-launch journey.

Need: Accountability partners

Throughout your re-launch journey, you need people that will be there to support you and constantly give you the push you need. They will get to know you well and be there to make you accountable. When the Amalekites came and attacked the Israelites at Rephidim, Moses told Joshua to go out with some men and fight the Amalekites while he stood on a hill with the staff of God in his hands. So Joshua went ahead and did as Moses said. Aaron and Hur went with Moses to the top of the hill. As long as Moses held up his hands the Israelites were winning, and whenever he lowered his hands the opposite happened. When Moses got tired, Aaron and Hur held his hands up – one on one side, and one on the other, while he sat down on a stone – so that his hands remained steady until sunset. This paved the way for victory as the Israelites overcame the Amalekite army.

Like Moses, you need people that can hold up your hands when you get tired or weary. You will need to choose your partners carefully and make a commitment to meet with them at regular intervals whether online or face-to-face. If you know a couple of other women who are keen to re-launch their careers, you can speak to them about joining your accountability crew.

Need: Coaches/mentors

These are people who support you and are there to help you not just to grow your skills but also to offer good counsel that helps you navigate through situations. They act as a sounding board.

Need: Comforters

These people calm you down when you have challenges. They are always quick to encourage you and give you a hug when you need one. My husband and my children have always been my main comforters.

Need: Clarifiers

Clarifiers help free you of confusion and help you to understand things better. They can possibly help you identify ways of achieving your goals. Such a person could be a career consultant or a coach.

Need: Challengers

These people mean well, are very blunt and will not hesitate to challenge you when need be, especially if they observe that you are doing something wrong. Challengers are few, especially when you are at the top, as not many people will be honest with you because of your status. We all need godly challengers.

Need: Collaborators

A person who willingly assists and co-operates with you to achieve your goal is a collaborator. This could be another woman who partners with you to set up a business or agrees to pick up your children or car share with you.

Need: Role models

These are people who have done the things that you are aspiring to do. If you can't find any, don't worry too much about this. However, if you know anyone, you'll benefit from reading their story to find out how they overcame challenges and kept going.

Avoid: Energy drainers

Energy drainers make you feel ineffective and frustrated. They range from those who constantly put you down, are very negative, filled with self-pity, to those who seem to have no other mission than to simply waste your time!

Avoid: Opposers

Whenever you have a dream or goal, there will be people who oppose you. Opposition often proves that you are doing something significant with your life. These people often put you down, and when they know what you're planning to do (e.g. set up a business or study for a qualification) they will say things like, "Who do you think you are?" "Do you know how old you are?" "Remember that you are black." "Do you think you can get any clients at all?" "You are the only woman." By the time they finish, you'll feel like giving up on your dream! Remember how Sanballat and Tobias opposed Nehemiah when he set out to rebuild the walls of Jerusalem. Whilst you do not need to be on the lookout for these people, you need to be prepared to deal with them when they show up.

DEVELOPING COMPETENCE

When I decided to switch lanes from the world of Industrial Chemistry to People Development, I explored different course provisions and made the decision to undertake a postgraduate diploma and master's degree in Human Resources Management. I believe that understanding what people need and knowing how to help them are two totally different things. This is a major reason why I have focused a lot on developing my skills as a professional Training and People Development Consultant. I am constantly in learning mode – taking classes, reading relevant publications and books, learning from mentors, attending useful events and doing independent research – so that I continue to build my competence and credibility. Confidence is vital to success, but I know that I also need to develop competence to truly achieve my goals. By focusing on developing my knowledge and skills, my competence levels have increased.

FACING REJECTION AND THE 'DASH'

I normally invite senior executives and top business people to speak at career networking events which I organise. Each time I am about to type an invitation letter or call these speakers, the fear of rejection sets in, which knocks my confidence big time. Over the years, I have become more confident and now understand that 'rejection' is part of life and does not mean I have a problem. The interesting thing though is that the majority of these executives accept my invitation. Constantly reminding myself that life is a short dash gives me a push and helps me to step out boldly. Life is 'the dash' between two dates – the day we are born and the day we die. I now recognise that realising my full potential makes the risks I take worth it. I wouldn't want to look back at the end of the 'dash' and say, "If only..." or, "Had I known..."

FUN AND RELAXATION

In 2011, after an accident, I started having panic attacks. This, coupled with high stress levels, led me to make a decision to have more fun and switch off from work (for minimum of a week) at least three to four times a year. I now find it easier to relax and have more fun with my children. There was a time when my kids had no proper routine, and this meant that they stayed awake till late at night. Of course, this made me really stressed because I didn't have enough time to rest. Once I managed to get the kids used to a routine and send them off to bed by 7:30 pm, it gave me the opportunity to have some 'me time'. I try not to miss my soothing night-time ritual of a hot bath which invigorates me and makes me feel better about myself. When my energy levels are high, I feel confident and alert to tackle problems.

Research shows that women are more likely to be affected by anxiety and depression. As women we have a tendency of looking after everyone else and ignoring our own wellbeing. I still find myself falling into this trap. Let's face it, it's not easy; modern day living brings mental and physical pressures. But it is crucial that we take good care of ourselves. Making small changes to what we do, what we eat and what we wear will impact on our health.

A SMART APPEARANCE

Any time I dress well or make my hair, I feel cool and confident. When I was getting ready to re-launch my career as an interim consultant, I refreshed my wardrobe with a couple of blouses, shift dresses, a black bag and two pairs of shoes. I had made a decision on the type of image I wanted to project, so I bought affordable clothes to help me achieve this plan. This enhanced my confidence. Can you imagine how good I feel when people comment on my appearance?

Face your fear

Courage is not the absence of fear, but the ability to face fear and overcome it. Fear can steal your dreams and cause you to give up on the vision that God has placed in your heart. You may be afraid of failure. You may be afraid of rejection. You may not want to make a fool of yourself. You may be afraid of trying because you believe you won't succeed. You may be worried about what people would say if you fail. If you give in to these thoughts and believe that you cannot get a particular job or run a business, you'll be right – and therefore unable to get the job or set up that business.

FEAR: False Evidence Appearing Real

Living fearlessly is not the same as never being afraid. The Bible gives us accounts of men and women of God who, though they were afraid, faced their fear head on. Take Esther, for example; she proved to be a woman of unusual courage and wisdom, facing adversity with a quiet confidence and trust in God. She called for a three-day prayer and fast before she approached the King. She acknowledged that courage alone could not help and asked her countrymen and women to intercede for her.

We must not allow fear to dictate our choices or to define who we are. Living fearlessly means standing up to fear and refusing to let it define and rule our life. It means refusing to settle for less than God's best for our life. It means refusing to take 'no' when we are sure the answer should have been 'yes'. God knew we were going to struggle with fear, and so to help us He filled the Bible with over 365 "Fear not..." or "Do not be afraid..." verses – more than enough for every day of the year!

Isaiah 41:10
So do not fear, for I am with you; do not be dismayed, for I am your God. I will strengthen you and help you; I will uphold you with my righteous right hand.

"Courage does not always roar; sometimes courage is the voice at the end of the day saying: 'I will try again tomorrow.'"
– Mary Ann Radmacher

"You gain strength, courage, and confidence by every experience in which you really stop to look fear in the face. You must do the thing which you think you cannot do."
– Eleanor Roosevelt

Faith that moves mountains

How long have you been talking about re-launching your career? I once met a lady who told me that for years she had been thinking about launching a particular product. After asking her a couple of questions, I realised she had not done a single thing to take her one step closer to her dream. I always feel like shaking people like this, to wake them up to see the possibilities that lie ahead of them. I wish they would start believing and applying God's Word. Instead of making progress, many women keep going around the same mountain wishing and praying for change. They would have made some progress if only they had taken prayed-on risks. Like the Israelites, many women keep wandering around in the wilderness because they have no positive vision for their lives and cannot see with eyes of faith. They just cannot see how they can re-enter the workplace after being away for ten years. Some cannot see how anyone will engage their services. Today the same words the Lord spoke to the children of Israel, when a journey of eleven days took them forty years, applies to us: "You have dwelt long enough on this mountain". It's time to choose faith over fear and move forward. Are you in?

Questions for reflection

Are you a diamond in the mud?

_____

What vision do you have for your life that has been covered by layers of mud?

_____

_____

_____

What constitutes the layers of mud around you?

_____

_____

What help do you need to bring out your sparkle?

_____

_____

_____

How can you get this help?

_____

_____

CHAPTER FOUR

Through God's Eyes

Women and work

Stories of working women in the Bible give an indication that God gives women skills and talents which He wants them to use in different spheres of life, including the workplace. I have also made a personal deduction, from reading the story of creation and the Proverbs 31 woman, that it isn't beneficial for us as women to place our jobs or businesses before the wellbeing of our families. God designed the woman to be a nurturer.

I have enjoyed learning from the working women in the Bible. Some of them are listed below.

DEBORAH[1] – JUDGE & PROPHETESS

Key characteristics:

- Determined
- Courageous
- Visionary Leader
- Risk-taker
- Worshipper
- Influential

During the time of the judges, Deborah arose as a judge and prophetess to lead the people of Israel against an enemy king that had cruelly oppressed them for twenty years. Deborah – wife of

---

[1] Judges 4-5

Lappidoth, mother not only to her own children but to Israel, prophetess, judge, and leader – shows us that women juggling their callings as wife, mother and leader have existed from the beginning. She also shows us that family and career can be juggled successfully.

LYDIA[2] – CLOTHES MERCHANT & BUSINESSWOMAN

Key characteristics:

- Enterprising
- Generous
- Hospitable
- Kind
- Influential
- Wealthy

Lydia was "a dealer of purple cloth"[3] from Thyatira. Purple dye was a symbol of power and honour in the ancient world, and it was the most expensive and sought after dye. While Lydia and a group of others were praying by the riverside, they encountered Paul and Silas. Paul shared the Gospel with them. Lydia opened her ears and heart and became the first European convert. She was baptized and then her household. She became a Christian and a marketplace influencer. The Bible states that she urged Paul to abide in her home and opened her home to Christian missionaries.

PRISCILLA[4] – TENTMAKER & CHURCH LEADER

Key characteristics

- Knowledgeable
- Loyal
- Reliable
- Industrious
- Generous
- Resilient

---

[2] Acts 16:13-15
[3] Acts 16:14
[4] Acts 18:2,8,26; Romans 16:3

Priscilla and her husband Aquila were tentmakers by profession. She is the classical example of a woman teacher in early church history. She was a celebrated missionary, church leader, and co-worker of Paul, who was generous in his recognition and acknowledgment of his indebtedness to her and her husband.

RUTH[5] – FARM WORKER

Key characteristics

- Dedicated
- Loyal
- Risk-taker
- Hard worker
- Obedient
- Resilient

Ruth was a Moabitess who married Mahlon, the son of Elimelech and Naomi – but Elimelech and his two sons died. When Naomi decided to return to Bethlehem, Ruth went with her. Ruth was a diligent farm worker who gleaned in the fields owned by Boaz. Her job involved beating out the grain and gathering it all up. To release the grain from the chaff and straw, workers used big forks or shovels to toss the mixture into the wind, which carried off the lighter chaff and allowed the heavier grains to fall back to the floor. Her hard work and obedience to her mother-in-law made an impression on Boaz, who eventually married her.

PHOEBE[6] – DEACON

Key characteristics

- Committed
- Trustworthy
- Respected
- Generous
- Wealthy

---

[5] The Book of Ruth, Matthew 1:5
[6] Romans 16:1-2

Phoebe is a woman Paul highly commended and respected. She was a "sister", "deacon" and "benefactor"[7] to the church at Cenchreae. She was a wealthy woman who served the church out of her means, just as the women in Luke 8 had served Jesus out of theirs. Paul trusted Phoebe enough to entrust his letter to the Romans to her.

HULDAH[8] – SCHOLAR AND PROPHETESS

Key characteristics:

- Literate
- Bold
- Pacesetter
- Influential
- Knowledgeable

Huldah was the last recorded woman prophet before Judah fell to the Babylonians. King Josiah sent the high priest to inquire of Huldah after a scroll was found in the temple. Huldah, wife of Shallum (who was the keeper of the wardrobe), verified that the scroll was the word of God and that its words would come to pass. She was literate and the first to declare scripture to be holy. Up until this time written words had not been declared to be the word of God.

These women inspire me because they chose to make a difference at a time when women were simply expected to remain in the confines of the home. They were everyday women who chose to trust God and to do something with what He had placed in them.

Deborah is a woman who truly inspires me. At a time when there was great oppression, this wife and mother challenged Barak and stood alongside him as Israel went into battle against King Jabin of Hazor, Sisera and their troops. Lydia used her wealth and hospitality to further the gospel of our Lord Jesus Christ. Rather than give up on life following the death of her husband, Ruth returned to work, her priority being how to care for the mother that her husband had left

---

[7] Romans 16:1-2 (NIV)
[8] 2 Kings 22:14-20; 2 Chronicles 34:22-33

behind. These women faced challenges and obstacles similar to what we are facing in our own time.

What God's Word says

When I go through difficult or challenging situations, I find that the Word of God gives me comfort and peace to carry on. The Bible contains many beautiful promises and stories. I am learning to read through the Bible and identify those that relate to the challenges I face. I learnt to do this when nothing else made sense to me. The Word of God is the most effective counterattack against the negative words that have been used to describe us by those close to us. Many women have a twisted view of who they are purely because of other people's careless and hurtful remarks. A woman who constantly hears her husband call her stupid may invariably feel stupid and incapable of making progress. A woman who grew up with abusive parents, where nothing she did ever seemed good enough, may find it difficult to set boundaries and may try to please everyone. In working with many women, I have seen first-hand the effects which negative remarks can have on individuals. I have been affected too, but here are some promises from the Word of God that have helped and transformed my life:

	Psalm 32:8
	I will instruct you and teach you in the way you should go; I will counsel you with my loving eye on you.
	Psalm 24:4-5
Confused and in need of guidance	*The one who has clean hands and a pure heart, who does not trust in an idol or swear by a false god. They will receive blessing from the Lord and vindication from God their Savior.*
	Jeremiah 29:11
	"For I know the plans I have for you," declares the Lord, "plans to prosper you and not to harm you, plans to give you hope and a future."

Tired	**Isaiah 40:30-31** *Even youths grow tired and weary, and young men stumble and fall; but those who hope in the Lord will renew their strength. They will soar on wings like eagles; they will run and not grow weary, they will walk and not be faint.*
Discouraged	**Psalm 42:11** *Why, my soul, are you downcast? Why so disturbed within me? Put your hope in God, for I will yet praise him, my Savior and my God.*
Feeling Oppressed	**Psalm 9:9** *The Lord is a refuge for the oppressed, a stronghold in times of trouble.*
Low in confidence / self-esteem	**Song of Solomon 4:7** *You are altogether beautiful, my darling; there is no flaw in you.* **Psalm 139:14** *I praise you because I am fearfully and wonderfully made; your works are wonderful, I know that full well.* **Philippians 4:13** *I can do all this through him who gives me strength.*
Afraid	**2 Timothy 1:7** *For the Spirit God gave us does not make us timid, but gives us power, love and self-discipline.* **Isaiah 44:8** *Do not tremble, do not be afraid. Did I not proclaim this and foretell it long ago? You are my witnesses. Is there any God besides me? No, there is no other Rock; I know not one.*
Sick	**Jeremiah 30:17** *'But I will restore you to health and heal your wounds,' declares the Lord, 'because you are called an outcast, Zion for whom no one cares.'*

Loss of income/ money	**Joel 2:23-26** *Be glad, people of Zion, rejoice in the Lord your God, for he has given you the autumn rains because he is faithful. He sends you abundant showers, both autumn and spring rains, as before. The threshing floors will be filled with grain; the vats will overflow with new wine and oil. "I will repay you for the years the locusts have eaten—the great locust and the young locust, the other locusts and the locust swarm—my great army that I sent among you. You will have plenty to eat, until you are full, and you will praise the name of the Lord your God, who has worked wonders for you; never again will my people be shamed.*
Ashamed	**Isaiah 61:7** *Instead of your shame you will receive a double portion, and instead of disgrace you will rejoice in your inheritance. And so you will inherit a double portion in your land, and everlasting joy will be yours.*
Experiencing Lack	**Psalm 23:1-2** *The Lord is my shepherd, I lack nothing. He makes me lie down in green pastures, he leads me beside quiet waters...*
Abandoned	**Hebrews 13:5b** *Never will I leave you; never will I forsake you.* **Isaiah 54:5-6** *"For your Maker is your husband—the Lord Almighty is his name—the Holy One of Israel is your Redeemer; he is called the God of all the earth. The Lord will call you back as if you were a wife deserted and distressed in spirit—a wife who married young, only to be rejected," says your God.* **Psalm 27:10** *Though my father and mother forsake me, the Lord will receive me.*
Lonely	**Genesis 28:15** *I am with you and will watch over you wherever you go, and I will bring you back to this land. I will not leave you until I have done what I have promised you.*

Ill-treated at work	**Psalm 66:12** *You let people ride over our heads; we went through fire and water, but you brought us to a place of abundance.* **1 Peter 3:14** *But even if you should suffer for what is right, you are blessed. "Do not fear their threats; do not be frightened."*
Guilty/sorry	**Psalm 86:5** *You, Lord, are forgiving and good, abounding in love to all who call to you.*

You are...

- ...a daughter of a King (Galatians 3:26)
- ...loved (Isaiah 43:3)
- ...beautiful (Psalm 139:13-16)
- ...free (John 8:32)
- ...victorious (Philippians 4:13)
- ...redeemed (Ephesians 1:7)

Embracing God as your Father

When the disciples asked Jesus how they should pray, Jesus responded with The Lord's Prayer. The disciples must have found the opening line "Our Father who art in heaven..." strange and unfamiliar, given that this was not the norm for them. Jesus was trying to take them into a deeper revelation of who God is to them.

I believe that one of the things that will boost our confidence and help us press forward is knowing that God is our Father and that He loves us so much. The Holy Spirit is the Spirit of revelation, and He will reveal the nature of God if we ask Him.

Questions for reflection

What does God's Word reveal about who you are?

_____

_____

_____

_____

_____

_____

What promise in God's Word will you hold on to from today?

_____

_____

_____

Prayer Nuggets

REPENTANCE

Pray for forgiveness of any sin that you're harbouring in your heart: anything of a wrong attitude; anything of unforgiveness or anger or bitterness towards your husband, a former boss or anyone else. Confess these before the Lord as sin.

Ask God to create in you the right heart. (Psalm 51)

WISDOM

Pray that God will help you to listen for His wisdom in the midst of adverse circumstances that do not have simple solutions. Ask Him to grace you with confidence and strength.

RESTORATION

Pray that God will give you double honour for every shame and reproach you have suffered. Pray that He will help you become the woman He created you to be.

Get up, Create, Break out

Create

When you create your
own opportunities,
you'll work for ever.

"For we are God's handiwork, created in Christ Jesus
to do good works, which God prepared in advance for
us to do."

Ephesians 2:10

Get up, Create, Break out

CHAPTER FIVE

Ideas Don't Stay Hot Forever

One afternoon, I had the opportunity of watching a couple being interviewed on Revelation TV. They spoke about how they had set up their business and the challenges they had overcome along the way. I was so inspired and decided to contact the wife and ask if she would take out time to meet with me. A few days later, I received a positive email response from her. I was ecstatic, and soon I was on my way to our first meeting.

I arrived at their community centre and was led to a room to wait for her. She appeared after about five minutes and we got talking straight away. She asked me a few questions to break the ice and then we got down to the real deal. Without mincing words, she asked me what I felt God was calling me to do. I had prepared some notes for the meeting, in which I had mapped out the three core areas I believed God was calling me to step into. She smiled, looked through my notes and zoned in on what I had written on training and developing women. Then she asked, "So, what's stopping you?" I can't remember my actual response but I know I mentioned something about money. She looked at me and said, "Money isn't your issue." After a couple of minutes of discussion, she instructed, "Choose a date for your first workshop." I was petrified but knew I had to do this, so I settled on a date and told her. She then went on to say she would be happy to feature as a guest speaker at my very first workshop. She explained that ideas do not stay hot forever and told me that if I didn't start, I would probably never do anything with the ideas rumbling in my head.

When I got back home, I went straight into planning mode as I had less than three months to plan this workshop. I decided to call the event 'Get up, girlfriend', and it would focus on empowering women to advance personally and professionally. I had recently married, and my husband and I were trying to save up as much as we could. I could not afford an expensive venue so I weighed my options and decided that this pilot event would be held in my local community centre. I was not sure whether anyone would attend, but I knew that I would never know if I did not try. I designed a flyer using an affordable online design and print service, and started emailing people in my network about the event.

In 2007, social media was not as popular as it is now so I relied on text messaging, word of mouth and targeted emails. The day of the workshop came and there were just over twenty women in attendance. Each woman was charged an attendance fee of £10 and was given a folder which included notes about the different sections of the workshop, inspirational quotes, activity sheets and action plan notes. In all honesty I made a loss, but I wasn't really bothered because I got much more than money could buy in return.

The feedback was fantastic, and those who attended asked me when the next one would be. I knew I was on to something. So following the success of this workshop, I started working towards another one. This time around, I decided to charge £30 per delegate and moved the venue to an affordable hotel. Again the feedback was fantastic and people started emailing me, asking me to run more events. At one point I even hosted a session in the function room of a restaurant and bar. The function room was free so long as people in the group ordered some food. This worked very well and helped to cut costs.

Running these first sessions boosted my confidence and propelled me to dig further and step into my destiny. If I hadn't make that first move, I would never have known the possibilities that lay ahead and my life would probably have taken another route. Anyone who sees me hosting career and business networking events now would not believe how petrified I was back then in 2007.

Every business, product or project starts with an idea. Some of the practical things that helped bring the ideas God gave me to life can be summarised as follows:

BE ACCOUNTABLE

By stepping out and meeting up with someone I considered a role model, I made myself vulnerable and accountable. This book would probably never have been written if I had not made myself accountable. When I realised I was dragging my feet, I told my friend about the book and asked her to keep challenging me to finish it. When I realised that this was not working for me, I decided to start planning the book's pre-launch event in advance. God had been nudging me to go back to hosting events for women, so I decided that the book pre-launch and the event for women would be held on the same day. I started praying and asking God for direction. Once God dropped the names of the speakers in my heart, I contacted them and told them about the event. I also told them that by God's grace I was planning to pre-launch my first book then. Now I had nowhere to hide; I had spoken and there was no going back. Setting a date for the pre-launch put positive pressure on me to complete this book.

When our ideas linger in the daydream state, there's a high probability that they will die there. No wonder people always comment that the graveyard is filled with lots of ideas – ideas of men and women that never saw the light of day! When you tell people you will do something, you will try as much as you can to do it. In 2009, I remember inviting a lady to facilitate a session at the first careers and recruitment event which I hosted for women. She told me she had started writing a book and planned to bring the books along to sell at the event. She set this target for herself in order to achieve the goal of writing her first book.

LOOK YOUR RISKS IN THE EYE

When I decided to re-launch my career, I was scared and had a series of sleepless nights. My husband and I talked about the things that could go wrong if I gave up my job. One Saturday morning, I had an interesting meeting with Mike. I was matched to him as a mentee through Kent Foundation's mentoring scheme. Before going for this meeting, I asked God to speak to me through Mike. During the meeting, Mike asked me to look at the potential consequences of giving up my job. I made a list which consisted of many pros and one main con: unguaranteed income. I looked at the positive things on the list, and all of a sudden not having a guaranteed income suddenly shrank in significance. The rest is history. Although I am not yet a millionaire, I can boldly say that God has been faithful.

HOLD ON TO A SCRIPTURE

I remember reading the stories of the twelve men who were sent as spies to Canaan. Of the twelve, only Joshua and Caleb believed that they could possess the land. Just before I gave up my job and re-launched my career, I drew strength and courage from Caleb's statement:

> **Numbers 13:30**
> *Then Caleb silenced the people before Moses and said, "We should go up and take possession of the land, for we can certainly do it."*

I meditated on the scripture over and over; and each time I was tempted to run and hide, Caleb's words echoed in my mind and pushed me to keep moving ahead.

DO-IT-YOURSELF (DIY)

I meet many women who complain that their companies do not invest in their development. Some get discouraged when their requests for funding gets turned down or when they are not given time off to pursue their personal development. My response is always same: use your annual leave days, try to save up, or ask the company to meet you halfway if possible. The truth is we as individuals are responsible for our career development. I am always intrigued to hear stories of individuals who had to take the bull by the horns and start their companies from scratch when no one else believed in their ideas.

Let's take the case of James Dyson who launched the 'G-Force' cleaner in 1983. No manufacturer or distributor would handle his product in the UK, as it would disturb the valuable market for replacement dust bags, so Dyson launched it in Japan through catalogue sales. The 'G-Force' cleaner won the 1991 International Design Fair prize in Japan. After failing to sell his invention to the major manufacturers, Dyson set up his own manufacturing company. If Dyson had given up because no one believed in his product, we would not know about Dyson vacuum cleaners today.

GIVE YOURSELF ROOM TO THINK

I enjoy taking out time just to think. Many women are so busy that they rarely have time to think and wonder. Allowing yourself to think is such a powerful thing. If you don't know where to start, I can suggest that you start by thinking of nature. I always give myself room to think about my ideas, and this often takes me on exciting journeys. Thinking makes the ideas feel and look so real that I just want to carry on and make things happen.

LET YOUR CRITICS MOTIVATE YOU

Early on in my career, when I was working as a support officer at a local authority, I applied for a job which was about five grades higher than the one I was doing. On finding out that I had applied for this job, one of the principal officers looked at me and asked, "What made you think you could get the job?" This guy had a reputation for discriminating against black women. Although he would never openly admit it, other colleagues were aware of his behaviour especially because of how he treated another black female agency worker. Rather than allow his comments to put me off, I resolved that I was going to get a job at that level (his level). A couple of months later, I applied for another similar role and got it. You don't want to know how cool I felt when I was invited to my former team's Christmas lunch! The guy could not look me in the eye; in fact he sat as far away from me as he could. This experience has taught me not to allow people's negative criticisms to weigh me down.

Questions for reflection

What idea are you sitting on?

_____

_____

_____

_____

What little (practical) steps do you need to take to make this idea reality?

_____

_____

_____

_____

_____

_____

CHAPTER SIX

What do You Want?

Many women struggle to answer this question. How about you?

I know that out of desperation to get back into the workplace after a long break, many women take up anything that comes their way. In most cases, these women settle for jobs that are way below their skills level and capabilities and get stuck in these jobs. Sadly this results in a life of emptiness and lack in fulfilment.

A deep sense of sadness floods my soul whenever I ask people what type of job they would like and they respond by saying, "Anything." I personally believe that this is a fundamental error which leads to frustration. This response shows that many neither know the talents God has deposited in them nor understand how to utilise these talents.

I am sure some of you reading this are thinking, "Veronica, get real!" The truth is I am being as real as you *can* get! Regardless of your present circumstances, a key step forward is to identify what you want to do. You need to have an idea of what God is flagging up as important in this season of your life. This will help you shape what you want, and you can then begin to play matchmaker between your aspirations and your skills, experiences and interests, in order to begin working towards what you want. Now, please don't get me wrong; this does not mean that you will get what you want immediately, in the way you think or on a platter of gold. In some cases, you may have to take a few steps backwards before eventually making your way back to where you want to go.

How flexible is your plan?

One of my very first professional mentors was an intelligent and hardworking man called David. I was matched as a mentee to David, who at that time was an assistant director of a public sector organisation, through a pilot inter-agency mentoring scheme at my workplace.

During one of my meetings with David, he drew a simple sketch to illustrate a potential route to achieving my career goal. Before drawing this sketch, he asked me what type of job I would like to be doing in ten years. At that time I was twenty-two and my response was that I would like to be a Director of Organisational Development in a public sector organisation.

Now, I recently turned thirty-one and I am the Director of my own consulting company which provides people and organisational development services. Whilst I am not the Director of a public sector organisation as I initially planned, having this plan kept me focused on developing the skills and knowledge required in this area of specialism.

You might be tempted to think that people become successful because they know their goals and follow a set of plans. But you'd be surprised to find out that many successful people don't stick to a conventional career plan. Having the understanding early on in my career that life could hurl several unexpected surprises in my path and that I may need to move backwards, sideways, etc. in order to achieve my goal, made it easy for me to adapt to unexpected challenges and situations. Successful entrepreneurs and professionals understand that life is constantly changing, so they are constantly evolving and positioning themselves to take advantage of opportunities that come their way.

Sometimes, in order to launch into what God has for you, you may find yourself taking steps that seem backwards from the world's perspective. A good example is the story of a woman who had a successful career built from years of working in one of the popular oil companies. Despite her success, she was not fulfilled because she had always felt it strongly from a young age that she was meant to work with children. Eventually, she gave up her job and registered as a child minder after doing a couple of childcare courses.

As I am growing in my walk with God, I am beginning to really understand that when we place our plans in God's hands, He has a way of turning things around for our good. He feels honoured when we seek His face before making plans and decisions. I am pretty certain that you feel delighted when your children seek your advice or opinion on the issues of life.

Seasons of life and what's important

After I had both of my children, I returned to full-time roles in the workplace. As my children grew older and had more awareness of things around them, I wanted to spend more time with them. So like many mothers, I desired a flexible working pattern that would still make effective use of my skills. I was working on a new business initiative when I had my first child and continued to work full-time for financial reasons. Less than two years following the birth of my son, I had my daughter and continued to work full time. My journey to work at that time took less than an hour, and this worked really well with the nursery's closing time. But deep down I knew I wanted more.

So what do you really want?

Knowing what you want is different from knowing what you don't want. When you only know what you don't want, your intentions aren't focused.

Let's take the example of Marie, who is tired of staying at home. She left the world of work six years ago after having her third child. Her last role was as an administrative manager at the local hospital. Now she desperately wants to go back to work but is not sure of what she wants to do. One thing she doesn't want is a boring job; she found her last role very routine-based and boring, a huge conflict with her bubbly personality and array of practical skills including cake baking, creative food displays, events planning, etc. She doesn't know which path best fits her skills and personality, and is also worried about things like money, childcare, etc.

Hoping to find some form of employment, she investigates a number of possibilities, but as soon as she reflects on potential obstacles or things that could go wrong, she decides that the path isn't for her and moves on to explore a new solution. Marie soon becomes frustrated, confused and discouraged, and wonders if she'll ever return to the workplace. Marie's actions aren't focused.

Now, what if Marie takes a step back to reflect on the creative skills that God has blessed her with? Suppose she begins to pray and look inwards to assess what she has going for her. A skills assessment will most likely reveal that she will be better off looking for a practical, hands-on role. Suppose she then decides to focus on something that revolves around baking as her main career goal, and as a temporary measure (because of her financial situation) she sets another goal of getting an administrative role in a hotel or related environment, as an entry path into what she loves. Other factors that may influence Marie's goal include working pattern, location, pay, etc. This will make her goals clearly defined.

- *Main goal:* Get a full-time job where she can use her baking skills (in nine to twelve months).
- *Temporary goal:* Get a full-time administrative role in an environment where baking or food preparation takes place (in six months).

Marie's alternative goal may be easier to achieve because she has relevant experience in this area. If she approaches this as a short-term means to an end, she is more likely to succeed because mentally she understands that she is only doing this temporarily until a relevant opportunity becomes available. Let's say she gets an administrative job in a hotel; her focus will then be to take advantage of any opportunities that will enable her enhance her skills or gain some practical experience which will add value to her CV.

A set of specific goals is much easier to achieve than a vague end goal like getting any type of job. Being focused on a set of paths gives Marie a set of actions to follow. As soon as she starts work, her goal may then culminate into actions such as:

- Find out about shadowing opportunities that will enhance her skills.
- Do the certificated e-learning Food Safety course.
- Volunteer to get involved in organising events which include food preparation.
- Do a short baking course at the adult education centre.

- Apply for a relevant (baking) job.

But how can she choose a path if she doesn't have an idea of what she wants to do? Once she is clear about what type of career she wants, she'll be in a good position to develop an effective job search strategy. Despite having a strategy, Marie will still need to be flexible and open so that she can embrace opportunities as they come her way.

The key is to be prayerful and proactive, rather than reactive – staying committed to taking small, manageable action steps toward a goal or dream. Remember, dreams and goals are at the top of a staircase – instead of trying to leap to the top, take it one step at a time.

Every skill counts

The world of work has changed. Years ago, it wasn't uncommon to see many people starting out in entry level roles in a company, working their way up the ladder in the same organisation and staying there until they were ready to retire. People had jobs for life; but not anymore! Our only security is in our unchangeable God who has designed us specially and equipped us with the skills we need for our life journey.

After studying a degree in Industrial Chemistry, my career journey took me back down the route of an administrative apprenticeship with a local authority in the Greater London area. I had always known that I wasn't cut out for the science world, and I spent five years studying a course I didn't really like. Not being one to give up, I looked for other ways to utilise and develop my leadership, organisational and people skills. I got involved in – and led – a number of groups that focused on empowering and educating people, and promoting justice. I was an editor-in-chief of a press organisation, a member of the student union, etc. During this time, I also held leadership positions in the church; one of my longstanding roles was as a youth leader of a local Pentecostal church. I developed excellent skills in planning and organising, presentation, problem solving, project management and continuous improvement. These skills prepared me for a subsequent youth co-ordinator role in another church.

As an apprentice in the training team, I was quick to notice that the core skills required in the world of training and people development were very similar to the skills I had employed in various leadership roles whilst at secondary school and university. These skills coupled with the quality-driven and research-based environment where I studied for five years provided me with a good foundation to build my career.

Many women looking to re-launch their careers don't do enough to reflect on their design and identify their core skills and strengths, and explore opportunities to further develop these. Do you know what your core skills and strengths are?

Once you can establish what you want at this stage, you can move on to the practical task of identifying the things you have, that can help you get what you want. What special skills and abilities have you developed – either before you left the workforce or in the years since then – that employers might want? These might include a few traits that you undervalue.

Once you have an idea of what you want to do, you can then move on to prayerfully explore your options and develop the necessary tools that you need to successfully launch out.

Career considerations

It is easy to feel that returning to work, starting a business or changing your job completely is right for you. It might be that your circumstances have changed (e.g. maybe your children have just started school). Maybe you feel you need to enhance your skills. Perhaps you are keen to start getting some income to support you and your children. Maybe you would like to get involved in some additional, stimulating activity. Or perhaps you just feel like you've held back for too long from doing what God wants you to do. Whatever it may be, are you really ready?

The exercise in the practical study guide at the end of this book will help you think through some of the areas that need to be considered before re-launching your career. Like me, it may even help you to make that long-awaited decision.

Questions for reflection

What do you really want?

_____

_____

_____

What is your definition of a successful career?

_____

_____

_____

How do you think God defines a successful career?

_____

_____

_____

Chapter Seven

The Journey of Discovery

I recently upgraded my Blackberry when the old one stopped working. Like many of us, when my Blackberry arrived, I totally ignored the manual and jumped straight to inserting the battery and getting it all set up, ready for use. As a result, I never got to fully understand the various functions, and this means I am not making effective use of my Blackberry. I won't be surprised if I find that my Blackberry can do certain things which I never thought were possible.

You have a responsibility to go to your manufacturer and ask about your functions. You were pre-designed for your purpose. We are all designed differently and for different purposes. Birds love to fly because they naturally have wings to do so. In a similar vein, most basketball players are naturally tall.

What is your design? Having an understanding of your inherent design will help you to stay in your territory. You will experience dominion when you operate in a terrain you were created for. Sometimes we can operate somewhere temporarily, but it doesn't necessarily mean we should stay there. This is why so many people never step into doing what they really should be doing – because they are comfortable where they are, even when they know it is not the right place for them.

Tools for discovery

As I mentioned earlier, the greatest problem of many people is that they have absolutely no idea what they should do. Many people have wasted years and skills that could have been put to effective use because of peer and family pressure. A very close friend confided in me that she suffered constant verbal abuse from her husband because she refused to re-launch her career in the finance sector. After a seven-year career break spent on looking after her children, her husband wanted her to re-train as a financial advisor, but she knew that this was not meant for her. All her life she had had a desire to work in a school and was not prepared to give up on what she believed was she was meant to do. My friend went through a lot of pain but continued to trust God for a breakthrough. She currently works in a part-time support role at a children's education centre and is now waiting and exploring potential opportunities for her next career move.

When I speak to many women who have no idea of what to do, I sense their frustration and hear the desperation in their voice. Many times, it's as though they want me to tell them what to do. I feel really privileged to be able to support women in identifying their vocation, and I recognise that this is something I was born to do. Based on my personal and professional experience, the predominant factors that influence the career routes of many women include divine revelation, skills and strengths profile, personality profile, qualifications, experience of adversity and available opportunities.

Some women continue in the same route based on the qualifications and skills they possess, or because of the opportunities open to them such as a job with their previous employer. Some decide to set up a business in response to a gap in the market. Others decide to set up not-for-profit organisations because of their desire to correct an ill or wrong in society.

Divine revelation

The greatest tool for those who have no idea of what to do is prayer. For many people this may sound intangible, but it is probably because they don't currently enjoy an intimate and close walk with God. I remember how depressed I used to feel when people would simply suggest prayer as a solution for everything. It has taken me time to grasp this important truth, but thank God that after many years of doing things in my own strength and reasoning, I now know the best way: prayer. In Psalms 32:8, God clearly states that He will instruct us and teach us in the way to go. And honestly, He is still our best bet; after all, He made us.

Although I have always sensed that I was called to have an organisation that provides services to women, it wasn't until 2012, when I had three clear dreams, that I became totally convinced that it was all part of my purpose and calling. The dreams boosted my confidence and strengthened my resolve to revisit what God had committed into my hands. In one of the dreams, I was drafted as part of a helicopter task force to go and save women who were being raped and oppressed. In another dream, I kept seeing mug shots of many women and saw the words 'missing in action'. When I asked the Holy Spirit what this meant in my dream, He responded that many of the women around me were missing because they were being suppressed and oppressed and so were not living in the real sense of the word. In the third dream, many women were locked underground in a dark place, and I was asking them what they were doing there. I kept telling them they had to come out towards the light and create wealth and opportunities for themselves.

Having these dreams was not enough as I needed guidance and direction on how to translate them into actions in real life. The truth is I did not get dreams on what to do next. Instead the Holy Spirit started dropping ideas and pictures into my heart. The Holy Spirit is the Spirit of revelation, wisdom and truth, and when we ask for His help, He will definitely show us the way – although, in most cases, we may have to wait, or the answer may not be in the form that we expect. Physical and emotional exhaustion can prevent us from seeing signposts which the Holy Spirit places in our path, or from hearing His direction. You may also have to put your feet into the water first, as the priests did at the edge of river Jordan (Joshua 3:15-16). This means you must choose to obey God's clear commands before you will see the path He wants you to take opened before you. God may ask you to learn a new skill, or He may ask you to help out in a group at church. If there is something God has been laying on your heart for a long time, irrespective of how unimportant this seems, you will benefit from taking a step of obedience as this is most likely part of your preparation for your next step.

Let me share an example of how divine revelation and guidance can lead one into an area where one has no real experience. A contact of mine told of how she was launched into the world of baking. Her Nan had just passed away so she went to her house to arrange and pack her belongings. Whilst doing this, she stumbled on a mixing bowl and spoon which she took home with her. A few weeks later she was missing her Nan and decided to bake a cake, so she used the mixing bowl and spoon. Soon she started baking every week, and people started commenting on how tasty the cakes were. Soon the orders came rolling in, and before long she started a cake business and moved into a shop on the high street. It is important to stress that she worked really hard, did some baking courses at her local adult education centre and read books on baking.

This shows that it is possible for one to re-launch into an area where one has virtually no prior experience. I cannot really give a systematic prayer guide, but I know that I have always asked God to show me the way. I used to be very religious, which made it difficult for me to hear God or see the signposts He placed in my path. Now I know the effect which a simple prayer based on God's Word has – it can bring great revelation.

Skills and strengths assessments

Skills assessment questionnaires are designed to give you information about your skills, interests and motivations in the workplace. These tools help you to think about the kinds of jobs that might be best for you. Some questionnaires help you to identify any skills gaps and find the qualifications that will help you to fill them. Some initially concentrate on general skills within different industries and then add more specialist skills once your results are revealed. I occasionally carry out an informal skills and strengths assessment of myself, in which I email people within my network and ask them to kindly tell me what they think my top three areas of strength are, and why. I always find it amazing that people usually come up with similar answers.

Personality profiling

My decision to re-launch my career as an Interim People and Organisational Development Consultant, whilst growing my organisation, stemmed largely from my desire to work flexibly and turn around short-term projects. I have always enjoyed pioneering and implementing new initiatives, delivering results and moving on to take on new challenges. Sadly most of my previous roles did not provide the best environment for this working style, and I found myself becoming more and more unfulfilled at work.

One day I had the opportunity of completing a personality profile questionnaire; the results confirmed some things I had always known about myself. Some of the words used to describe my personality type included:

- Places her whole body and soul into a project.
- Pragmatic, quick and flexible.
- Joins teams and projects with enthusiastic optimism and a conviction to succeed.
- Relishes new activities and new challenges.
- Can be an outstanding entrepreneur, able to swing deals and kick-start enterprises in a way no other personality type can.
- Establishes objectives, routes, purpose and benchmarks.

My job at that time was extremely routine-based and boring, so it was obvious that I was going to struggle in such an environment.

Personality profiles usually measure how an individual interacts with others, communicates, makes decisions and responds to crises. They may also assess an individual's learning style and give an idea of the jobs best suited to their personality. Profiling provides a snapshot view of the preferred behaviour that comes subconsciously to most people. This is the behaviour with which they are 'comfortable' and can sustain for long periods of time. The means by which this behaviour is measured is a questionnaire which asks the respondent to choose the behaviour most and least like them. The questionnaire is not a test – as there can be no right or wrong answer. It is simply an estimation of the individual's typical way of dealing with the world. The most commonly administered personality profiles are the Myers-Briggs Type Indicator, Keirsey Temperament Sorter, Enneagram of Personality, DISC Profile Personality Test and the Hartman Personality Profile.

Experience of adversity

Many of us will go through a trial or period of adversity at least once in our lifetime. The only thing is that the situations and degree to which we are impacted will be different. Although we would rather avoid them, we have to remember that our greatest growth in life often come from those times we experience adversity, choose to overcome the adversity and allow our trials to make us better.

For some women, the adversity and trials don't just make them better; the trials propel them to take meaningful actions such as setting up a charity, launching a campaign or even starting a business. Some make the decision to work for organisations that are involved in some way, in helping people going through a similar painful situation to what they or someone close to them experienced. Let's take the example of a lady whose father died of cancer when she was very young. Her painful situation influenced her decision to develop a career as an oncologist.

It is true that some of our greatest ministries/careers will stem from our deepest hurts or pain. I remember coaching a woman who had a desire to work with young people. When I probed further, she explained that as a teenager growing up, she had felt alone and had received no guidance and support from the adults around her. I know another woman who set up a charity to campaign against female genital mutilation. Having experienced this and some other forms of abuse as a child, she made up her mind to do something about it. For many working women, the maternity period offers ample time to reflect (amidst dirty nappies and sleepless nights, of course), and this explains why some women choose to re-launch their career by setting up charities or social enterprises after a career break.

It is not uncommon to see women who have businesses or hold down day jobs and run charities alongside. I would say this applies to me too.

Questions for reflection

What has God laid on your heart (this could be something you think about consistently, dreams you've had, etc.)?

_____

_____

_____

What are your top five areas of strength?

_____

_____

_____

In which sectors/areas of work can you effectively use your top three strengths?

_____

_____

_____

CHAPTER EIGHT

Which Way?

Without a doubt, your ability to successfully re-launch your career has much to do with your ability to figure out exactly what you want to do, and to pursue that goal with resilience and determination. Here are some of the ways women are re-launching their careers:

THE VOLUNTEER

Volunteering is rewarding and has helped many women gain experience and confidence. It's a great way to give your CV a boost, get a reference and fill gaps in your work experience. You can also try out different types of work to get a taster – which can really help you if you're looking for a job or want to change direction.

After a ten-year career break, Carly put herself forward as an administrative and receptionist volunteer at a popular business centre in Medway. She put in extra hours and always had a smile for visitors and the business owners who occupied the centre. Not long afterwards she was headhunted by the owner of a solicitor's firm based in the centre and now works as a Legal Secretary.

Many organisations offer voluntary work placements and will usually respond positively when approached. For medium-sized and large organisations, it is advisable that you contact the HR department, and for small businesses you can speak to the Managing Director or a named employee directly. I have found voluntary placements for many women by simply researching about individual organisations and calling them to make enquiries. I have also had success stories where voluntary placements have led to paid jobs. One such story is that of Darcy, who landed a permanent, paid support worker role in a care home after a four-week voluntary placement.

THE STUDENT

The decision to retrain can help you update your skills and gain a qualification or certificate. If you decide to study at a university or college, you will benefit from a range of career and employability services provided by the institution. You will also benefit from networking with your tutors and other students. If you are after a short course, your local Adult Education Centre or college is sure to have a list of various courses that may interest you. There are also a number of organisations providing distance and online learning courses.

I met Rebecca when I exhibited at her university's Careers Day and was intrigued by her story. After a ten-year break as a stay-at-home mum, she decided to undertake a degree and fulfil her dream of becoming a bioscientist. When I met her, she had just finished her second year and was exploring paid internship opportunities.

THE EMPLOYEE (INCLUDING CAREER RE-ENTRY PROGRAMMES)

An obvious route for many women is to return to the job they were doing before they took a career break. The difficulty many women encounter is in proving to organisations that their skills are still relevant. There are some career re-entry programs at some universities, government agencies, companies, professional associations and foundations worldwide which offer women the opportunity to refresh their skills and re-enter the workplace. Some of these programmes are listed at the end of this book.

THE CONSULTANT OR FREELANCER

Some women prefer to re-launch as a consultant or freelancer, focusing on their core area of specialism. A consultant is usually paid to provide professional or expert advice in a particular field or specialty e.g. management consultant, marketing consultant. A freelancer is a person who works independently, selling work or services by the hour, day, or job, with no intent to pursue a permanent or long-term arrangement with one single employer e.g. copywriter, graphic designer, photographer etc. In most cases the freelancer works off-site using different tools and resources. I have re-launched my career both as a freelancer and consultant. As a freelancer, I worked as an associate trainer for some training organisations and was paid a daily fee for delivering soft skills training. As a consultant, I am recruited by client organisations to work on specific projects within an agreed timeframe. Once the project is finished, the relationship with the client ends – at least until the next project comes along.

As I mentioned in an earlier chapter, I chose this pattern of work because it offers me the flexibility I need in this season of my life and suits my personality profile. The variety of projects I work on keeps me going.

The Entrepreneur

Many women choose to start their own businesses following their career break. The majority of them start with little or no capital and take different forms e.g. self-employment, partnerships, limited companies, etc. There has also been an increase in the number of female social entrepreneurs who start a business with the aim of achieving a desired social change.

The Portfolio Worker

Portfolio careers are usually built around a collection of skills and interests. With a portfolio career an individual does not have one job but does multiple paid activities at the same time. It's the opposite of having one traditional full-time job. These multiple activities may include part-time employment, freelancing, temporary jobs, and self-employment, which when combined could give the equivalent of a full-time position. Portfolio careers offer flexibility, variety, and freedom, and this is why this option appeals to many skilled mothers who use portfolio careers to juggle their time effectively. A very good example of someone with a portfolio career is one who works as a part-time Business Development Manager for a local recruitment firm, does some freelance recruitment work and provides occasional corporate HR consulting to some organisations.

THE MINISTER

In response to God's call, some women decide to start what many term 'ministries' following a stay-at-home period. I know some people make a great distinction between working in the marketplace and running a ministry. But for me there is really no distinction as I believe that God expects us to transform wherever we are with our light. This means that wherever we are, we are effectively called to minister God's love and grace.

THE HOME-BASED OR REMOTE WORKER

Whether you call this remote working, teleworking, or home working, it's definitely on the rise. Call centres, banks, software companies, law firms and PR agencies are among the types of organisations that offer these opportunities. Many women choose this type of work, mainly because of the flexibility it offers. Companies like 'Arise' offer home-based customer service and call centre opportunities. The rise in online shopping has also led to an increase in the number of people who run online businesses. Take the example of Joanne, who started an eBay business selling children's clothing and accessories following the birth of her last son, and says it is really convenient.

Questions for reflection

Which of the above re-launch routes appeals to you?

_____

Why are you thinking of going down this route?

_____

_____

_____

CHAPTER NINE

What is in Your Hand?

One of the greatest privileges God offers us is the partnership we have with Him. Not only are we His partners, we were made in His image and designed to be creators like Him.

In the beginning, when God created the world, He spoke and carried out some actions before things were put in place. I am always amazed when I meet Christians who believe that all they need to do is pray and – pronto – all they want will come their way. It is wishful thinking to simply expect God to do things for us without us doing anything. During one of my counselling sessions with Pastor Bennett, he explained that God has never excluded men and women from anything He does and that any faith that makes God responsible for everything without our input is an irresponsible faith. I agree!

One of the crucial things I have learnt in my re-launch journey is the need to prepare for God-ordained opportunities, and one of the best ways to do this is to develop the tools I need and refresh the skills I have.

Finding and getting jobs

"There are just no jobs out there," lamented Elizabeth for the fifth time in a row, during a CV writing group session. I asked Elizabeth to tell me how and where she had been applying. Her response did not surprise me. I hear similar responses every time.

Elizabeth had previously worked as an accounts payable clerk before giving up her job to raise her sixteen-month-old baby. For the past three months, she had been applying for jobs online by relying on search engines to bring up relevant jobs and then submitting her CV. She explained that out of frustration she had even started applying for *any* job. She was visibly upset when she explained that a cleaning company had sent her an email saying she did not have suitable experience for the cleaning job she had applied for. She felt really insulted and found it hard to believe that the cleaning company could send her such a response. I calmed her down and then went ahead to show the group why Elizabeth was not achieving any success with her job applications.

I would like to share some of these reasons with you:

NO JOB SEARCH STRATEGY

First of all, Elizabeth clearly had no real strategy and was using a scattergun approach which meant she never actually hit her target. After carrying out extensive homework on herself to establish who she is, what she has to offer and what type of jobs to apply for, Elizabeth would have benefited from taking a candid look at the local job market to establish the best sectors to apply for. It is relatively easy to find out what is going on in one's local area. The Internet provides a wealth of information about the sectors that are performing well, and the Government's statistics website provides Labour Market Information (LMI) for different areas. Keeping a job search log will help you to keep track of the applications you have made.

INEFFECTIVE JOB SEARCH TECHNIQUE

Like many people, Elizabeth relied heavily on putting key words into search engines and then applying for the jobs that came up. This is one of the top ways that people search for jobs, but sadly it's also one of the least effective. Can you imagine how many people Elizabeth would have been competing with? Elizabeth would have fared better if she had used a combination of the following:

- Direct applications on employer websites (with a focus on companies performing well). Women who are re-launching their careers after a break are better off making direct applications to employers instead of relying on recruitment agencies who generally prefer to put forward candidates with the most up-to-date skills and experience.

- Using Yellow Pages to identify potential employers and calling them to enquire about any current or upcoming vacancies.
- Asking for job leads from people in her network.
- Registering with sector-specific job sites.

GENERIC CV FOR DIFFERENT JOBS

Like Elizabeth, many people send off one standard CV for different jobs. This approach wastes not only the individual's time, but also the employer's time. A targeted and well adapted CV will increase the probability of you being invited for interviews.

POOR CV

When I looked at Elizabeth's CV, I could not hide my shock. Her CV was poorly laid out and did not create a good impression. I used to run a job board and was often amazed at the very poor quality of some candidates' CVs.

OUTDATED SKILLS

Elizabeth admitted that a lot of the jobs advertised required some skills and qualifications which she did not possess, or which she needed to brush up on. Many re-launchers will benefit from updating their skills to ensure they are well positioned in the job market.

ATTITUDE

I am sure you are wondering why I included 'attitude'. Many people behave as if the world owes them something and so are overconfident and cocky in their approach. Elizabeth was one such person. I told her the truth in a nice and warm manner. The great thing was she listened and promised to improve in this area. Unknown to many people, their negative attitude can come across even through written communication. For some it's subtle, for others it's very obvious. I have had feedback from employers who explained that they did not shortlist some candidates because of how they came across in their CVs or application forms. Many employers also base their decisions on their perceptions of their interaction with candidates during an interview. By getting our attitude right, we invariably make ourselves more attractive to potential employers or business investors and partners. Your biggest asset is your attitude.

The hidden job market

It is a well-known fact that most employers never advertise their vacancies. In fact some people believe that over 70% of jobs in the UK are not advertised through the popular job channels. Imagine you are a small business owner with a thriving restaurant serving Mediterranean dishes. Your business is expanding and you are moving to a larger space that can accommodate twice the number of customers that you currently serve. You now need to recruit more staff. How will you do this? Am I right in guessing that you'll probably inform your existing staff about your requirements and ask them to mention the upcoming vacancies to their friends and contacts?

Some employers prefer not to use the popular channels because they can be expensive, lead to more administrative tasks and are generally time consuming.

Everyone has a hidden job network, but not everyone uses it. You can gain access to hidden jobs via:

- family and friends
- neighbours
- previous employers, associates and colleagues
- previous or current teachers or trainers
- your local church
- your women's group
- places you have volunteered
- work placement
- networking events
- competitors of former employers
- speaking to those currently doing the type of job you want to do
- directly approaching employers
- your local gym
- your social club
- your local café or restaurant

- former customers of your previous employers
- professional associations
- alumni associations
- children's school or nursery (asking teachers or nursery staff if they know of any vacancies)
- social media (posting a private question on the Facebook page of the company you are interested in, using LinkedIn strategically, etc.)

Marketing & PR tools

What influences you to buy certain products? Imagine that you have a company and your product is yourself. Now reflect on the fact that you are responsible for marketing and promoting your product. What will you do? What will your PR campaign look like? What tools and techniques will you employ to ensure that you present yourself in the best possible light?

You probably have a lot of transferable skills and experience, and all that you need is the ability to showcase these in a way that positively reflects what you can offer a potential employer. Those who have a business or community idea will benefit from being able to articulate what may appear to be an intangible concept. How proud God must be to see His children showcasing and using what He has put inside them. This is where the tools below can be of immense help.

YOU

You are your best PR tool. Your appearance, your mannerisms, your character, your body language, your timekeeping, your attitude and what you wear all give a certain impression of the type of person that you are. Every time you meet someone new, that person forms an opinion about you. This is very important, especially because of the general belief that first impressions are difficult to undo.

THE INTERNET

There's so much we can do with the Internet. It opens up many opportunities for us, so much so that we don't have any excuses whatsoever not to be doing something tangible about our re-launch plans.

NETWORKING

A general consensus about networking is that it creates a pool of contacts from which you can draw leads, ideas, referrals and information for your job search. So where or how should you start? People say that it matters who you know. This is really true so the first person who should be in your network is God!

If you have been out of work for a while, think about your career options and make a note of the people that may be able to point you in the right direction. Don't worry if you can't remember everyone. This list will only serve as a guide, as you are bound to come up with more names as you go on.

Building contacts and keeping in touch with contacts that you have means that you have a wider choice available. If you have been out of touch with some people, don't let that stop you from re-establishing contact when you start your job search. To jumpstart a network that's out-of-date, start by asking people whom you have stayed in touch with for some of the contact information you need. Everyone you speak to will have had to look for work at some point in their career, and most of them will be happy to help.

Professional associations can give you access to people who may work for, or have contacts within, companies you want to work with. Join professional associations or groups in your industry and then look for their events that you can attend. If you've been in a more senior executive position, consider volunteering to speak or facilitate at events or offer to serve on committees for professional associations. Get to know people in your field and allow them to know you. Make your interests, experience and talents known.

Informal networking can also help. Many informal networks are not registered anywhere and you will have to do some digging to find them. Most local councils have information about existing business networks, and there is usually a local Chamber of Commerce with events open to members and non-members. It's important to note that just about anyone can become a contact – friends, friends of friends, relatives, neighbours, former colleagues, members of clubs or societies, a former boss, old school mates, church members, etc.

Don't forget the six degrees of separation[9]. You don't know who knows whom. People will only give you advice or referrals when they have an idea of what you are looking for. Here's a word of caution though: the biggest mistake is to simply go around asking people for a job instead of establishing relationships and asking for advice. It is also important for you to be prepared to help others.

Alumni associations offer another way to make great connections. You can try contacting the Alumni Relations Office of your alma mater to find out about any upcoming events and groups or its membership database.

Online social networking sites such as LinkedIn and Facebook are good ways to find old connections and can help your job search. Personalise your invitation requests so that the recipient can remember who you are. Once you've re-established your relationship, you can also view the friends of your connections and request an introduction to people at companies that interest you.

Don't forget that networking is a give-and-take experience. When you hear of something that may be of interest to others, be sure to pass it on. Always offer to return any favours your contacts provide, and be sure to contact them even at times when you don't need their support. Even if nothing happens immediately, stay in touch and continue to pass on information to others.

Networking takes time to develop. Keep the fire burning; you don't know where the opening for your next job will come from.

ELEVATOR PITCH

As a jobseeker or business owner, an elevator pitch is like a TV commercial for yourself or your business; it sums up why you're awesome and why the employer/client should engage your services. The key point of your elevator pitch is not to ask the person to do something for you; it's to tell that person what you can do for him or her.

Take a minute to think about how you introduce yourself. Do you present yourself in the best light possible? Do you translate your skills

---

[9] Six degrees of separation is the theory that anyone can be connected to any other person through a chain of acquaintances, in a maximum of six steps. It was originally set out in 1929 by Hungarian writer, Frigyes Karinthy in a short story called "Chains".

and achievements into simple words that anyone can understand? Frame your pitch along these lines: "This is what I can do for you based on my experience and educational background…"

Your elevator pitch can also double as your response for the "Tell me more about yourself" question during a job interview. If you are looking for a job, repeating your elevator pitch to yourself at the start of every day can be a quick but encouraging reminder of why you are the best at what you do.

How to prepare a good elevator pitch:

- Pick the statement that says the most about you and what you want to be, and make it the highlight of your pitch, right after your introduction.

Example

Hello. My name is Sade Williams. I have success-fully managed Information and Systems Analysis teams in small businesses and most recently in a global IT agency where I identified cost savings of over £250,000 in one year. I would like to add value to your organisation in the position of a Senior Systems Analyst as I have done for previous clients.

- Focus on mastering the key points of your elevator pitch, rather than memorising a fixed script. That way, it's easier to customize it to suit the situation and the person you're talking to, and you'll sound more natural too.
- Read your pitch out loud in a natural tone of voice and speed (don't rush!) and time yourself to make sure it is under thirty seconds. Edit out unnecessary words if you have to, read again, and revise again until it sounds right.
- Practise speaking your elevator pitch out loud, first to yourself. When you're comfortable with it, practise it on family and friends, and ask them for feedback on the content and your performance
- Deliver your pitch in a confident manner. Look the other person in the eye, smile and offer a firm handshake.

When you call someone, state your name, your goal and mention the name of the person who referred you. People are busy so keep your conversations short.

CURRICULUM VITAE (CV)[10]

Your CV is one of your most important marketing tools. Its main purpose is to get you an interview. Its chances of success or failure depend entirely on how far it meets the criteria and bias of the person reading it. When producing a CV, many re-launchers...

- ...fail to identify what the employer is looking for.
- ...underestimate and undersell what they have to offer.
- ...fail to provide the right evidence to support the skills and competencies.
- ...fail to layout the CV in the best way possible.

Below are a few tips that will help in creating a performance-based chronological CV, which is the format that I generally recommend for those re-launching in the same (or a similar) sector:

- Get yourself in the right state of mind. Reflect on your previous achievements and goals.
- Put yourself in the shoes of the intended employer. You are not writing a CV for yourself; you are writing it for the employer, who may have to browse through hundreds of CV's. You want your CV to be the one that is engaging, concise and, most importantly, one that shows the value you can add to their organisation.
- A CV should not be written in the first person. No recruiter or future employer wants to read a CV full of "I did this" and "I did that". Furthermore, writing a CV in the first person often leads to it becoming too verbose.
- *Header.* Create a header for your CV which includes your name (in a slightly bigger font), address and contact details. Ensure that your email address is professional e.g. veronica@gmail.com or veronica.anthony@live.com. Do not use something like mamarocker@yahoo.com or sexymama-121@hotmail.com!

---

[10] For some useful resources including CV templates, visit *www.getupcreatebreakout.com*

Veronica Anthony

212 Lakeland Avenue, Canterbury, Kent CT1 2DS

T: 01235 675 234   M: 07900 89 6040

veronica@gmail.com

- *Personal Profile.* Think of this as a headline to a major front page news story. What is going to grab that reader to want to read further? A CV has to *grab* the reader from the very beginning. If a CV does not convey a match within ten seconds, an employer or recruiter will move to the next candidate. Come up with four to six lines customised to match the job description and hot buttons of the employer or recruiter. Tell them who you are, what you do and how you do what you do immediately.

Example

Client focused business development manager with transferable skills acquired in marketing, property and media sectors. Delivers outstanding results, builds excellent stakeholder relationships to provide advantage for the company and uses strategic thinking, inspiring leadership and financial awareness to achieve longer term objectives.

- *Key Skills and Achievements.* Using a couple of bullet points, you can include your significant skills and achievements that you know are sure to 'wow' an employer, before going on to your career history.
- *Career History.* This should start with your most recent employment – detail the job title, the company and the period you worked there (use a consistent format for your dates). A recruiter should be able to look at it and know what you did at each job and how long you were there. Identify the key roles and responsibilities that were associated with each of your roles, and then pick out five to six specific examples that show how the company benefited from your performance. Use action words to make a favourable impression on the recruiter or potential employer but don't overdo this. Accomplishments

should be quantified in pounds or percentages. If you increased productivity of the department then state from what to what. 1%? 10%? 90%?

Example

Targeted local B2B segment and developed a network of business contacts that helped increase company sales by 50%.

If you cannot quantify your achievements, try as much as you can to reflect the results achieved by your performance.

Example

Promoted a positive image of the organisation by answering the telephones professionally and accurately relaying messages to the senior management team.

For roles/jobs from over twelve years ago, you can create a 'Previous Career History' section and briefly summarise them in one or two lines. You should only include them if they are directly relevant to the job you are applying for or if you have been out of work for a long time. Where you have had similar roles in different organisations, you can group these together to avoid repetition.

- *Education, Training and Qualifications.* Start with the highest level of education obtained and work back. Keep it brief. Don't forget to include memberships. List relevant training courses too. For certain roles that require specific qualifications, e.g. hairdresser, beautician, accountant (qualified), project manager, you may benefit from highlighting your qualifications at the beginning of your CV (after your profile) or you may want to include a reference to your qualification in your personal profile.

- *Additional information.* Keep brief and factual. Use this as an opportunity to reflect your personality and interests. If you are the chairman of a society it shows leadership qualities. If you organise fundraising events it shows you are great at planning, organising and networking. Your involvement in sports suggests you are fit and healthy, etc.

- Check for spelling mistakes, typos and grammatical errors. If there are careless errors, it directly reflects on you.
- Keep your font simple and easy to read on a computer screen. Do not use italics or extremely difficult to read fonts like Edwardian Script. Font size is just as important as style. 8-point fonts are too small to read, even for Superman!
- Most recruiter database systems prefer CVs in Microsoft Word format, but it is worth also sending a PDF document along if possible.[11] Do not send your resume in a ZIP file; a CV is not meant to be a bulky document.
- Review your CV and show it to someone who can give you honest and constructive feedback. Before you send off your CV, do remember to name the document appropriately when you save it e.g. *Veronica Anthony CV* or *Anthony, Veronica CV.*

Things to avoid:

- *Hiding your career breaks.*
  Use the CV as an opportunity to demonstrate the things you have done which are relevant and applicable to the workplace. For example, raising £10k as the leader of your women's group shows that you have good commercial and leadership skills, whilst setting up a holiday club at your local church shows you are creative, resourceful and enterprising. As another example, Yvonne took a career break to become a personal carer to her mum who had cancer. She didn't get paid for it, but it added a lot to her CV when she wanted to re-launch as a support worker. Word of caution: don't spend too much time going into too much detail about everything you have done in your career break, as this will take a lot of space. Remember that most employers only spend a few

---

[11] Some computers need proprietary software (Microsoft Word) to view Word documents, whereas PDF documents can be viewed on any machine with the free Adobe Acrobat Reader. Word documents are reformatted when they are opened by the user's current software and may not look the same way they did when you created them, whilst PDF documents always retain their layout. A Word document with a spoiled layout might be frustrating to someone reading a large number of CVs.

seconds checking a CV, so you want to ensure that your CV grabs their attention. If you cannot think of any transferable skills gained during your career break then state it simply as a career break with the dates.

- *Burying important pieces of information.*
  No recruiter has the time to play Poirot or Sherlock Holmes to figure out your background, relevant skills and achievements. So make sure it's obvious.

- *Stretching the truth or telling an outright lie to land a job.*
  Half-finished degrees, inflated education, inaccurate dates to cover up job-hopping or gaps of employment, etc. are some of the common lies which candidates include in their CV. There's a difference between blagging, and using professional and business language to showcase your skills and achievements. Only write achievements in your CV that you are confident talking about at an interview.

- *Assuming everyone understands company jargon and acronyms.*
  As much as possible use language that someone outside your previous company would easily understand.

- *A lengthy CV.*
  Your CV should be ideally two pages long. In some cases, it may extend onto a third page.

A skill-based (functional) CV will be generally more appropriate than a performance-based, chronological CV, if you are seeking a change of profession or a significant change in industry. It may also be ideal if you are looking for a very senior or specialist consultancy role or have only worked in one specialised industry for most of your career.

For a skill-based CV, the Skills Profile / Summary sections should come after the Header and Personal Profile sections. You need to identify the core skills needed in the industry you want to move into and give specific examples of how you have used this skill in previous roles. Please note that the CV format used in the creative industries is different. As the name suggests, there's a need for creativity. The Internet has various examples of how individuals have landed jobs by using super-creative CVs.

Get up, Create, Break out

Please note that the tips provided in this section are by no means exhaustive – just a few pointers in the right direction. As a CV writer, I know that despite reading books and attending workshops, some re-launchers still struggle to put together a CV. If this applies to you then you probably need to engage the services of a professional CV writer. The 'What you've got going for you' exercise in the reflective guide at the end of this section will help prepare for your meeting with a career coach or CV writer.

Email signature

You can make the most of your email by creating a 'signature' that describes what you do in a few words at the end of every email you send. Some people include a link to their online profiles too.

Career letters

The three common letters used by jobseekers are cover letters, speculative letters and application form letters. Cover letters, as the name suggests, are normally sent as the cover for CVs when applying for an advertised job. In this letter, you need to refer the employer to key sections in your CV and explain why you are the best person for the job. CVs do not necessarily need to be sent with a cover letter, but it can work in your favour.

Speculative letters are used to enquire about potential vacancies when no jobs have been advertised. These letters are very effective job search tools as they will show that you use your initiative and can help you access the hidden job market. In sending speculative letters, it is important for you to address your letter to a named individual such as the Managing Director, HR Manager or Recruitment Manager. I have been successful in getting consulting assignments by sending speculative emails, so I highly recommend that you use them.

Application form letters are laid out similar to covering or speculative letters, and are sent to a company who are advertising a vacancy to request for an application form as specified in the job advertisement.

APPLICATION FORM

Most public sector organisations use application forms, which helps them to obtain more specific information about individual applicants. The following key points will help when completing applications:

- Always read the entire document before you begin your application, and take note of any key requirements.
- It is advisable to complete paper applications using block letters and black ink.
- Only provide information which is relevant, and do include impressive achievements.
- It is advisable that you type out your supporting statement in a Microsoft Word document and attach it to your CV. Don't forget to include your name in the footer of this document and ensure that you write, "Please see enclosed statement" in the box provided for the supporting statement, so the employer is aware.
- Your supporting statement should not just be a paragraph but should be comprehensive, detailing how you meet each of the essential and desirable requirements outlined in the person specification.
- Do not include your CV unless specifically requested.
- In completing online applications, you should press *Save* (if it exists) at intervals so you don't lose what you have written. You may want to copy the questions into a Microsoft Word document and then copy and paste back into the application form once you have finished.
- Present information consistently, and get someone to check it for you.
- Always keep a copy of the application form so you can use it to prepare for the interview.

SOCIAL MEDIA

LinkedIn, Facebook, Twitter, About.me, MySpace and Plaxo – they are all 21st century social networking sites which stormed the Internet not too long ago. More importantly, they are key job search tools. The one you use will depend on your sector and personal circumstances. Facebook is particularly great for those thinking of setting up a small business or becoming self-employed such as a driving instructor, beautician, caterer, decorator, etc. Most big organisations use their Facebook page to drive customer engagement and promote their offerings. Aspiring artistes use e.g. MySpace, YouTube and Vimeo to share videos of their work, or SoundCloud and ReverbNation to share music.

LinkedIn is no doubt the most important tool for business communications after emails. As a consultant, I use LinkedIn to make solid connections with other professionals and keep abreast of what's going on in different organisational and career networks. Whilst I have never really used LinkedIn to actively search for opportunities myself, my profile helps to boost my credibility, and I use it to source for top speakers and trainers.

Here are a few tips when using social media:

- Keep your profile fresh and current.
- Update your status line often and thoughtfully.
- Make useful connections – build your network carefully.
- Be careful with what you put online – it is difficult to erase things once they are on the Internet.
- Adhere to the site's rules, and use whatever is appropriate to the site and your situation.
- Be courteous and respect others.
- Do what you can to make your profile or page stand out.

Like so many things in life, you need to research more about the different sites and use the one that best fits your current situation.

BUSINESS PLAN

Many potential start-up businesses are intimidated by the prospect of writing a business plan. But it is not a difficult process – and a good business plan focuses the mind and can help to secure finance and support. The business plan will clarify your business idea and define your short and long-term objectives. It provides useful benchmarks to help monitor your progress and is also useful in convincing key stakeholders, e.g. your bank, investors and suppliers, to support you.

The following are the key sections of a business plan:

- Executive Summary
- About the Organisation
- Strategy
- Markets and Competition
- Sale and Marketing
- Operations and Delivery
- Management and Personnel
- Funding and Finance
- Appendices

OTHER TOOLS

There are many other tools such as business cards, websites, etc., and I have only featured some of the most common ones. In addition to marketing tools, it will be beneficial if you know how to use the main tools of trade associated with your specific sector. For example, if you are a project manager, it will be an advantage if you know how to use project management tools; a trainer is expected to know how to use Powerpoint, etc.

The Rule-breaking God

I know I have spent time highlighting the need to have great tools. However, God can work wonders even when tools are absent or an individual doesn't have the necessary qualifications for the job. I have seen this first-hand, and this is why I am always quick to point out that God's favour supersedes all other tools. In the first chapter, I shared how I was contacted to lead on delivering career and outplacement training to senior managers and employees of some public sector organisations. The truth is I had never done this before and the managing director had never seen my CV when she called me. It was simply a God-connection. I love these connections because they make it obvious to all concerned that God Himself is in control. Tools are great but not sufficient on their own. God's favour will open doors of opportunity that tools cannot open. God doesn't play by our rules, and He can do whatsoever pleases Him. Moses stammered, yet he led a nation out of Egypt. Joseph was a slave in a foreign land, and by divine arrangement he became second-in-command.

It is true that to survive in the marketplace, who you know matters. Based on my personal experience, I can boldly tell you that nothing beats knowing the God of wonders, the Master Planner and Divine Connector.

Our God is indeed a rule-breaker. His ways are not our ways. However this does not give us an excuse to be sloppy or careless with what He has given us.

Theresa's story

Theresa re-launched her career as a Sales Manager after an eight-year career break.

After spending eight years as a stay-at-home mum, I was eager to return to the workplace. With my qualifications and more than ten years of professional sales experience, I figured I would secure a new position quickly by browsing through the popular job boards and sending out my CV.

Six months later, with no interviews to show for all my efforts, I decided to change my approach. For years I had nurtured the idea of re-launching my career as a Sales Manager for a nearby furniture company. I knew that the position did not exist and that there was no vacancy, but that did not deter me. I did some research and found the contact details of the furniture company's Director. Armed with this, I decided to take the direct email approach. Despite this bold effort, the weeks rolled by and still there was no response.

Knowing fully well that many companies in the local area attend networking events, I began to search for network membership listings and events on the Internet. My search paid off, and I found details of a networking event which the furniture company Director regularly attends. Luckily the event was open to non-members, but I had to pay a registration fee. Before the event, I carried out more research about the company and prepared an elevator pitch. A day before the event my nerves took over. I became very scared, but my husband was quick to reassure me. I knew I had to forge ahead with the plan. It was too late to turn back now.

At the event, I deliberately sat at the same table with the Director. My opportunity finally came during the speed networking session. I was shocked at how bold I was when I finally got to speak to him. I explained that I had been trying to reach him to ask if he needed a Sales Manager for his company. His response was unexpected: "You've been stalking me. I remember reading your emails. Are you able to come to my office tomorrow afternoon for an interview?"

The rest is history. I still work in the same furniture company.

Go prepare!

> *To every [woman] there comes a time in [her] lifetime, that special moment when [she] is figuratively tapped on the shoulder and offered that special chance to do a very special thing, unique to [her] and fitted to [her] talents. What a tragedy if that moment finds [her] unprepared or unqualified to do the work which could have been [her] finest hour.*
>
> – *Winston Churchill (feminised for the purpose of this book)*

Preparing for interviews

Preparing well before your interview provides the following benefits:

- It helps to boost your confidence.
- It gives you the opportunity to sell yourself in the best way possible.
- It creates a good impression. When you have prepared well it shows you are serious and have a commitment to the company and the position you are being interviewed for.
- It displays enthusiasm and shows that you are proactive.
- You will be better prepared to deal with difficult or unexpected questions.
- If you have prepared well and don't get the position you want, at least you know you have put in 100% effort, which is important for reviewing your performance and planning the next course of action.

This table provides guidance on the range of issues to look at.

The Role	The Person	The Company	You
Examine the job advertisement closely. What does it say about the role?	Does the person specification fit your description?	What type of company is it? Where is the company located?	What do you have to offer? What are your Unique Selling Points?
Check the story behind how the role was created.	What skills are they looking for?	What is the size of the organisation? What are the pros and cons of this?	Compare your skills with those in the person specification. Is there a good match?
What experience is required?	What would you be expected to achieve in this role?	Are you aware of any changes in the company?	Begin to identify some potential questions that they may ask you.
What is the job title?	Will this be a standalone role or will you be working in a team?	Who are their main competitors?	Ask someone else to help identify potential questions.
What type of environment is it?	Do you have the required skill and expertise?	What style of language is used in the company's marketing materials? Their website and corporate plan will give you an idea. Corporate plans can normally be found on the company website under the 'About us', 'What we do' or other relevant section.	Prepare responses to the questions by writing out practical examples of what you've done in previous roles and life situations.

Responding to questions

Rather than list other practical things which you need to do to prepare, or the do's and don'ts which you probably know already, I would like to discuss an important part of interviews which many re-launchers find daunting: responding to questions.

You do not *answer* questions; you *respond* to them. This means that you control the information that you give. So use your responses to put across the information about yourself that the employer wants and needs to hear. I recommend that you use the 'STAR' approach:

S: Situation	Describe a specific situation
T: Task or problem	What challenge did you face?
A: Action	What action did you take?
R: Result	What resulted from your action?

Example 1

Q. *"What sort of product manager would you say you are?"*

A1. *"I am good at identifying and designing profitable products. I also manage relationships effectively".*

This answer is basic and most candidates respond this way, but look how much stronger the following is:

A2. *"When I was at HSBC, I liaised with business partners, asset managers and frontline staff from 8 partner organisations and managed the development of a regular premium savings product from conceptualisation through to implementation and ongoing monitoring, which yielded a profit of 70%. I believe this shows that I am a strong results-oriented product and project manager, and have the skills to build and manage effective stakeholder relationships."*

Example 2

Q. *Give an example of how you've used your communication skills at work.*

A1. *"I am good at communicating with customers and providing good customer service when they come into the store."*

This answer is basic and most candidates respond this way, but look how much stronger the following is:

A2. *"As a sales assistant at Dorothy Perkins, I maximised product sales through personalised customer interactions. Armed with a smile and warm approach, I stood at strategic locations in the store which made it easy for me to provide customers with information about our products and promote available offers and incentives."*

Whenever you describe some action you have taken or experience/skill that you have, always ensure that you go on make the links and to stress the benefits or results. Some employers say it is helpful to start off with a theoretic definition and then go on to respond using the S-T-A-R approach.

Market research

When I started my first business, I analysed information too optimistically and did not carry out a thorough market research. I paid a price for this and eventually made a decision to close the business. If you intend to set up a business, researching your potential market is essential. Your first step is to identify your potential customers. It is likely that you already have an idea of who your customers could be. For example, if you are thinking of setting up a cleaning service, busy parents and professionals would be two possible market sectors.

WHO

If you will be selling to individuals, you need to know their sex, age, occupation, income and lifestyle. If you will be selling to businesses, you need to know their size, industry type, buying patterns and service requirements. You also need to know what features are common to all your customers and who makes or influences the buying decision.

WHAT

Now that you have some information of who your customers are, you need to explore and find out what they buy and also an idea of the quantities that they buy. You should have an idea of what will be your top selling product.

WHEN

If you are planning to start a rental or BBQ business, then you know that potential customers will engage your services more during the summer period. This will enable you to plan effectively.

WHERE

Do you have an idea of where your customers prefer to buy from? Shops, market stalls or online?

WHEN

What will be unique about your products or services, and why should customers come to you?

The practical stuff

So, you've done a lot of things to prepare for your re-launch, but what about preparing yourself, your husband and your children? What are the things you need to do to ensure that the transition phase is as smooth as it possibly can be? Here are a couple of suggestions:

TALK TO YOUR HUSBAND AND CHILDREN WELL IN ADVANCE

Ask God to grant you favour with your husband and children, and then let them know why you want to re-launch your career. If your children are still young, do let them understand the value of work. You can even get creative and tell them the story of creation and the origin of work.

Once you've determined your schedule, take out time to discuss all necessary details with your husband and children. Make changes in your children's routines well before you begin working. For example, you may want your children to start at the after-school club a week before you return to work. You may also want to dedicate a special day for family time and make this really special. One of my friends told me that in her house Friday is known as film night. On this day, she doesn't cook and everyone bunks downstairs with nibbles or takeaway. My husband and I used to take the kids to the cinema on Saturday mornings, although this changed when the kids started swimming because their lessons were on Saturday morning. You don't have to do anything expensive. We took advantage of Cineworld's Movies for juniors where each member of the family pays 90p or a £1 to watch a film (applies only to films at 10am on Saturday mornings).

GET THE BEST CHILDCARE YOU CAN AFFORD

For most women, this is often the most difficult bit. I cannot overemphasise the importance of praying and asking others for recommendations before making a decision. And even after you do, you still need to ask God to watch over your children. Your local Family Information Service (contact details available online) can provide you with a list of childcare providers in your area. You may also want to consider the type of environment that will suit your child's personality and interests.

ACCEPT EARLY ON THAT YOU ARE NOT PERFECT

I struggled with this one. When I returned to work, I developed a schedule for my children, taking great care to split their activities so that if they learnt about shapes today, they would practise their sounds the next day. I developed a food timetable and even made a rule to serve a three course lunch every Sunday afternoon. We had to have fruits in the fruit bowl at all times so the kids could enjoy a bowl of chopped fruits every morning. As a clean freak, I kept a tight rein on where things were kept as I could not stand the house being a mess. Do you get the picture? I was trying to be superwoman and have it all!

I became stressed, and little things started getting to me. I will not lie and say I have completely changed, especially with regards to keeping the house tidy. My children (bless them) know they have to tidy up their toys as soon as they finish playing to avoid Mum's tongue-lashing! However I have relaxed in many other areas: plates can stay unwashed overnight; I no longer have to hand-wash every white shirt; we don't always have to eat fresh food; and takeaway and pizza won't kill. Oh, and it's okay if the fruit bowl stays empty for a couple of days, and no one will die if we don't have desserts. I now accept that things can be 'good enough' instead of 'perfect'. I am learning from my mistakes and thus able to take time out just to relax and enjoy life better. Please give yourself a break; your family will thank you for it.

PLAN YOUR WARDROBE.

Do you have suitable clothes? If you don't, try and get some. You don't have to spend a lot. There are budget-friendly fashion retailers, and you can get good quality, pre-loved clothing at very affordable prices.

GET YOUR CHILDREN INVOLVED IN RUNNING THE HOUSE

You may want to come up with a timetable of activities and highlight who is responsible for what. Don't feel guilty about this. It will make your children more responsible. Children like to help when asked. My children stress this point constantly.

BUDGET WISELY

This is important because there's usually a gap between when you start work and when you get your first salary. If you are on benefits, you may want to approach the local job centre to find out about any available incentives or support. As a last resort, you may want to borrow from close friends or family and pay it back as soon as you get paid. Don't forget to inform the relevant government agencies of your change of circumstances to ensure you are not overpaid any tax credits.

PLAN YOUR TRAVEL

If you'll be doing the school run, plan when you have to leave the house, etc.

Don't underestimate what you have

There are numerous examples in the Bible which reveal that God wants us to take our rightful positions as creators, and use the things which He has placed in our hands to produce the things we need. When you trustingly give what you have to God, you are basically saying, "Lord, I ask for your favour and trust that you will breathe upon my CV, project, speculative letter, business plan, etc." When

Get up, Create, Break out

God breathes upon something, it multiplies, flourishes and succeeds. The little boy's five loaves of bread and two fishes became food for thousands when he offered it to Jesus. Moses' rod became a supernatural tool used by God to perform wonders. Ezekiel had to prophesy before the bones came to life. What do you need to present to God today?

Questions for reflection

What have you decided to do now?

_____

_____

_____

What do you have to offer?

_____

_____

What tools do you need to develop?

_____

_____

What things do you need to put in place before you break out?

_____

_____

_____

Prayer Nuggets

REVELATION

Pray that God will lead you and direct you in all your ways. Ask the Holy Spirit to reveal God's perfect plan for your life. Ask Him to show you what you can do with what God has placed in your hands.

FAVOUR

Ask God to favour you and bless the work of your hands. Ask Him to lead you and open doors of opportunities for you.

PROTECTION

Ask God to watch over your home. Ask Him to protect you, your children and your husband.

Get up, Create, Break out

Break Out

Nothing must hold you back now.

"In the same way, let your light shine before others, so that they may see your good works and give glory to your Father who is in heaven."

Matthew 5:16 (KJV)

Get up, Create, Break out

CHAPTER TEN

Moving Mountains

What is your motivation?

Why do you want to do what you want to do? My own answer can be summed up as follows:

- To fulfil my God-given purpose.
- To create opportunities for others.
- To leave a godly legacy.

Joseph, Daniel, Moses, Esther and Paul all had God as their ultimate motivation, and this is why their lives had such great impact. When I read their stories, I see faith, risk, rejection, failure in the eyes of the world; for some I see hardship, trials, courage, opposition, perseverance, faithfulness, and determination. We have to ask, why were they able to stand strong in the midst of challenging situations and intense opposition without compromising or giving up? The answer is, their motivation was God and glorifying Him. Think of how different the lives of these people would have been if their goal had been the approval and praise of man.

Expect challenges

As you prepare to launch out into the marketplace, you will benefit hugely from making one big decision, which is to settle the issue of *why* you want to do what you want to do. If I know I am going to buy a dress at a particular shop when I leave my house, I won't bother about going into any other shops along the way. Yet when I leave my house and I do not know what to buy or where I will make my purchase from, it can take me hours to buy just one dress because of my indecisiveness. As daughters of God, we are not immune from challenges, but we can choose how we respond to them. So we can expect that things could go wrong: husbands may let us down; bosses may treat us harshly; and we may be under-appreciated, forgotten, used, misused, taken for granted, and dismissed easily. Yet, we know that we are loved by our heavenly Father who is always happy to help us and has great plans for us. If your motivation is not to glorify God through what you want to do, then you will really struggle. But if you have settled the issue of why you want to do what you want to do, then your joy and purpose will not be diminished even in the midst of intense challenges.

How big is your God?

Know that God is working His plan out perfectly. If you do not have a God that is able to do anything, then your life will be a miserable mess. I think a lot of people believe God can do anything but don't really believe He can do things specifically for them. Every time I think of my God-given vision, I sometimes panic and get overwhelmed by the magnitude of it all, until I suddenly remember how big my God is. It's good to have the right perspective.

When I made up my mind to set up my own consulting company, things went from bad to worse. I felt as if I had made a terrible mistake when no work was coming in. I think about Joseph and how he went from a pit to slavery to prison. Things kept getting worse and worse, but Joseph remained faithful to the Lord.

Make a decision today that no matter how things turn out, you will still honour God. If we are going to be women who glorify God, we need to trust Him in all situations. Too many women focus on the approval of others and not of God. Too many women focus on being recognised and celebrated instead of simply living for the Lord and His glory. We should never leave God and His glory out of the equation. What is your motivation? I pray this both encourages and convicts you.

What do you see?

Do you see opportunities or are you constantly looking at the limitations and obstacles around you? I once heard the story of an entrepreneur who made shoes. He travelled to a remote village in Asia because he thought there may be a market for his product there. He got off the plane and immediately noticed that no one was wearing shoes. He called the factory at home and said, "Cancel the order right away. There's nothing here for us because no one wears shoes." Then a second entrepreneur with the same kind of business made the same trip, got off the plane, and also noticed that no one was wearing shoes. She took out her phone, barely able to contain her excitement, and instructed her plant manager to double the size of the order. "There is an incredible opportunity for us here," she said, "because no one is wearing shoes." For me this story says it all. Is the glass always half-empty or half-full in your eyes?

Who art thou, mountain?

Perhaps the real reason that you are not reaching your goals in life is... *you.* A lot of re-launch plans do not see the light of day because of self-sabotaging actions and mindsets. Think of the woman who whines about not getting a job when she consistently sends off poorly written applications, or the woman who complains that her husband is not supportive of her plans even though she is constantly disrespecting him. It is obvious that these women's actions are sabotaging them – they have become their own worst enemy. Sadly many people in this situation are clueless about what they are doing wrong. Take a candid look at your life to identify whether your actions are sabotaging your plans.

When your husband has other ideas

So, you've got this wonderful idea of what you want to do at this stage of your life. You've managed to silence the negative voice that keeps trying to discourage you. Everything looks great, until you speak to your husband about your plans. What can you do if your husband has other ideas about what he thinks you should do? Or perhaps you know he will disagree with your re-launch plan because he normally plays the submission card and likes controlling you. How will you deal with this? Do you give up your dreams or ignore him? There are no easy answers, but you must take intentional actions to ensure that this conflict does not develop into isolation. Here are a few suggestions:

KNOW AND UNDERSTAND HIS DIFFERENCES

Like couples everywhere, your marriage is made up of two people with different backgrounds, habits, expectations and personalities. Guess what? You are bound to have conflict. It's unavoidable. Your husband's perspective and identity will be greatly influenced by his background so it will help you to have an understanding of why he comes up with certain ideas which you may find unbelievable. Remember that he may find some of your own attitudes and ideas unbelievable too. For example, a man who grew up in a family where his mum never worked may find it difficult to understand why you want to go out and work, when he is able to provide for the needs of the family. Once you understand where he is coming from, you know he is not deliberately trying to be difficult but simply saying what he believes is right. This will help you not to feel victimised.

SHOOT ARROWS OF PRAYER

I learnt a key principle when it was almost too late, and this is the importance of praying before sharing whatever God has laid on my heart with my husband. The power of prayer goes beyond what I can describe in words. Prayer paves the way and can steer the heart of your husband in the direction that God wants for your family. Prayer can also bring more revelation about your re-launch plans. I have spoken to women who have clearly heard from God about the pattern of work to adopt and the best time to re-launch. Others received clear direction about what to launch into. Sometimes, after praying and asking the Holy Spirit for wisdom, some women receive clear direction about how and when to approach their husband to tell him about their plans. Esther could have gone straight to the King when she heard about Haman's plans to destroy the Jews, but instead she chose to tell him after a dedicated time of prayer and fasting. Furthermore she didn't just tell him straightaway, she prepared a banquet for him. Your husband is your 'king' so ask God for wisdom on how best to broach the issue with him. You can do this even after a first failed attempt to get him on your side.

DEFEAT SELFISHNESS AND PRIDE

At the beginning of this book, I explained how my resolution to become successful stemmed from the things I saw around me whilst growing up as a child. I did not even know one man who was faithful to his wife, and to make matters worse, I saw first-hand how women were treated as second-class citizens; this made me angry at both men and God. I did not understand why God would make men the head of the home and watch them oppress women like that. Obviously I had a distorted and unbalanced opinion which led to my making a vow that I would be successful so I wouldn't have to depend on a man. My thinking was that women were treated shabbily because they depended on men. Thank God for Jesus!

When I got married, I unknowingly brought this misguided thinking into my marriage. Many women will never admit to being selfish or proud because they do not think that they are. It took the Holy Spirit working on my heart to reveal the state of my heart to me. My question to you now is: are you being selfish? Have you assessed your husband's viewpoints honestly? Are you proud? Remember that you are a team and are supposed to work together for the well-being of your marriage and home. This applies to men as well, as there are many husbands who focus on pursuing their career ambitions to the detriment of their family life. I always reflect on what someone once told me, that when people die their workplace carries on like nothing happened and it is usually their family members who feel the pain most. They are also the ones who are normally there when we experience illness and personal tragedies. A humble and selfless heart will likely cause your husband to listen carefully to your plans.

LET GOD'S WORD SET YOU FREE

Some women believe that they will be stepping out of God's will if they return to the workplace because of their husband's opposition to the idea. God established order in the home by making the husband the head of the home, and God's original plan is that marriage should be a partnership of two people who value each other and both have an input into decision making. God expects wives to be submissive and to trust the decision of their husbands based on the expectation that the husband will care for his wife and think of her best interests. Unfortunately, this isn't the case in some homes, and trusting the decision of the husband may make a wife go against God's Word. Let us consider the situation of a husband who tells his wife not to work and yet does not give her money to look after herself and the children. Trusting his decision that she should not work will be inappropriate because, if she does not work, she and her children will suffer. Many women are living in bondage because of wrong and unhelpful interpretation of the scriptures. No two situations are the same, so do take a candid look at yours and ask the Holy Spirit to give you the wisdom you need specifically for your situation. You may need to set boundaries and stand your ground to realise your plans. In all that you do, check that you are doing what is godly.

SPEAK THE TRUTH WITH LOVE AND RESPECT

Even if you may dread his rejection, disapproval or anger, your husband needs to know the truth about your plans. Focus your conversation on telling him why you want to re-launch your career, rather than trying to force him to agree with you. Don't lash out in anger as this will make him defensive and angry and will result in the situation not being addressed. Instead, share your feelings and ideas in a loving way that is less likely to provoke arguments. Many women withdraw when their husbands are not keen on their re-launch plan. This is counterproductive and will make things worse. Watch your body language, tone of voice and choice of words to avoid any form of disrespect. Sometimes you may need to tell your husband that what he is doing is wrong, but you need to approach him in a way that will make him realise that you love him enough to tell him the truth.

Here are six points to consider before discussing with your husband.

What is the problem and why is it a problem?

Be clear and specific about what is making you sad.

What needs to change?

Think of constructive suggestions that can help resolve the situation.

What would you like?

Be clear about what you would like, instead of simply moaning about the current situation.

When should you speak?

Choose your timing carefully. Always think about when would be ideal to have the conversation with your husband, and do work out what you are going to say in advance. You can request to speak to him in advance and agree on a time when there will be no distractions.

How should you say it?

It is important that you do not give in to anger. Here's a good example of how to open the conversation: "When you discard my plans to work as a student support manager at the university, I feel discouraged, unloved and unsupported. I would like to share the reasons why I am interested in pursuing this career route with you..."

What about afterwards?

At the end of your conversation, summarise your points clearly and ask for your husband's agreement. Listen patiently if he has any suggestions and carefully repeat your points. Don't forget to let him know how happy you are, and thank him when he agrees to your plan.

SUGGEST A WIN-WIN SITUATION

I have spoken to a few women who decided to change the pattern of their work or timing of their re-launch plan to reach a compromise. Let's take the case of Rhonda whose husband works five days a week from 10 am to 6 pm. When she told him she was planning to return to work after a one-year break spent looking after their daughter, he was worried about their daughter's welfare. He grew up in a close-knit family and was never placed in a day care or nursery provision; hence he recoiled at the thought of leaving their daughter with strangers at such a tender age. Rhonda took her time to convince her husband that nurseries were okay. After having an honest discussion with her husband, Rhonda made the decision to wait until their daughter turned two before going back to work. Her husband felt touched and went on to fully support her re-launch plan when she was ready. Marriage is a partnership where both parties work together towards a common goal. It is not about who wins; it is about winning together.

Mr Culture

Man: How are you doing?

Me: I am fine, thank God.

Man: *[He goes on to talk about his business interests.]*

...

So tell me, I hear you work for yourself. What exactly do you do?

Me: I work as a career development consultant, supporting people back into work.

Man: Oh that's really good. How come you only talked about what *you* do? You didn't mention your husband. I find that really interesting...

This is an excerpt from a true conversation I had with a man at a family event. To say I was shocked is an understatement. The truth is I made excuses and went on and on about how my husband and I do everything together even though we work in separate fields. I even talked about how he supports me in my work and how I support him with his. I was trying to justify why I didn't talk about my husband when I was asked what I did as an individual. I was glad that my husband was not nearby and did not hear the man's comments.

For those who find this shocking, welcome to the 21st century living experience of many women from certain cultural backgrounds. Although the specific situations that these women face are different, the issue is the same: in these types of culture, many of the men believe that women should neither be seen nor be heard.

Living in the Western world brings anguish for certain women who are married to men from specific cultural backgrounds. For these women, their husbands do all they can to enforce their cultural traditions and ensure that the women understand who is boss. One Sunday I attended a church at which there was an open discussion about marriage and people were invited to give their comments. One married man stood up and said, "I don't understand the problem with many of these women. They think that because they are in the

West, they can behave anyhow. When I was growing up, my mother never dared speak where my father was…"

I have heard heart-breaking stories of the ill-treatment that some working women suffer at the hands of their Christian husbands. I believe God weeps when He sees the pain His daughters are going through. Once I was overwhelmed with so much pain about this issue and asked the Holy Spirit why many women were suffering badly and what I could do to help. The only response I heard was, "Tell them I love them."

If you are currently facing this mountain, there are no easy answers. One thing I want to make really clear is that God loves you and has not abandoned you. The issue of culture and tradition is a complicated one. In many cases, there are deep-rooted, foundational strongholds that need to be dealt with prayerfully, particularly because many of these cultures have their roots in occultism.

It is sad that many people profess to be Christians but do not live the Kingdom culture, which is God's way of doing things. My experience of working with women who are affected shows that the majority of them are often isolated and suffer from very low self-esteem. I always encourage anyone planning a re-launch, regardless of the challenges, to get connected with other people. Reach out to friends, family and your church family. There is strength in numbers, and God does not want us to be lone rangers. Even when Jesus sent His disciples out to preach the good news, He sent them in twos. Whatever you do, please reach out to other people. Joining a support group can be a significant step in learning to believe in yourself; when you hear the stories of other women, it will no doubt teach you one or two things and help you understand that you are not alone.

I also recommend that you get wise counsel from a godly pastor. I have used the word 'godly' because not all those who profess to serve God do so, and what hope will you have if you end up with a pastor who has a similar mindset to your husband? Professional counselling may also be required in some cases, although you will need to pay for this. Ask the Holy Spirit for wisdom, and ask Him to lead you to the right person or support group.

It is Christ-like to persevere during trials, but this does not mean that you should put yourself in harm's way. You need to apply godly wisdom and must learn how to stand up for yourself in the right way.

Above all, pay attention to your physical and mental well-being – your health and safety is really important.

I have recapped the above points below:

- Always remember that God loves you.
- Ask the Holy Spirit for wisdom.
- Reach out to other people.
- Get wise counsel.
- Apply wisdom.
- Stand up for yourself in a respectful way.
- Take care of your physical, emotional and mental health.

The Proverbs 31 man

Everyone knows and talks about the Proverbs 31 woman, but what about the Proverbs 31 *man?* What impact does being a successful working woman have on the dynamics of one's relationship with one's spouse? By being successful I do not necessarily mean that you earn more than your husband (although this may be the case). It could be that based on the nature of your career, you are better known or even more popular than your husband.

There are many men that have no problems with their wives being more successful than they are. But I am sure that if you speak to these men you will find that they have a healthy self-esteem which is rooted in God, and they understand that their wife's success is automatically their own success too. Unfortunately, many people (both men and women) do not have healthy self-esteems. This probably started when they were young and could be as a result of their father or mother walking out on them, or perhaps they did not feel loved by one or both parents, or maybe they grew up in an environment where their voices were never heard. I struggled with low self-esteem issues and I know how destructive this can be.

A successful working woman married to a man with a low self-esteem will probably have a tough time at some point, not because the man does not love her but because he suffers from a low self-esteem and is secretly crying out for help. The problem is that because he is crying in secret, no one can hear him, not even his wife. He keeps his pain and struggles bottled in, until one day the lid goes off and out comes an unexpected outburst directed mainly at his wife. What causes the lid to come off could be something seemingly insignificant such as a subtle comment by a friend or relative, that he is not good or 'man' enough, or it could be something major. The woman shocked and hurt by his behaviour and outburst lashes back in anger and things spiral out of control.

It took the help of the Holy Spirit to open my eyes and teach me by taking me behind the scenes, back into the past of many individuals. Only then did I begin to understand the reason for the many problems that couples face. Even where a man has a healthy self-esteem, the external environment does not help – and no doubt the enemy is after marriage. He understands that if the home is destroyed, society has no hope. Some women are also filled with pride and resentment, and sometimes it will take only the help of the Holy Spirit to reveal who we really are. Only then can we cry out to God, like David, and ask Him to create in us a new heart.

If you are reading this and this resonates with you, the only tangible suggestion I can give you is that you should go on your knees and ask the Holy Spirit to give you the wisdom you need to build your home (Proverbs 14:1). As you pray for your husband, you will also need to take practical steps to safeguard your home. This is where only the Holy Spirit can help you. I have not done a great job in this area, but I trust that God will make me the wife He wants me to be and bring full restoration.

The balancing act

I recently declined an opportunity to travel to Korea for three weeks. The offer looked attractive as it was to be an 'all expenses paid' trip with spending money provided. Not only was this a sensitive time in my marriage but there was no way I could imagine leaving my young children for over three weeks. Not long after this, I was contacted about another opportunity to source for trainers for a summit which was to be held in Hong Kong. Although this too did not materialise, God used this to teach me a basic principle, which is that 'not all that glitters is gold'; the fact that a door is open does not mean I should walk through. Some job offers and business deals may look attractive, but they may not necessarily be part of God's plan for our lives.

As working women, we will always have to make choices. I have learnt the importance of doing what I call a Spirit-sense-check to find out which path to take. In some cases, the answer will be very obvious, but some can be blurred and will take the help of the Holy Spirit to show the way. I have personally made a decision about the types of consulting projects to take on because I want to have ample time with my children.

I must be honest in saying that I don't always spend time with my children. I sometimes give them things to do e.g. painting, building blocks, playing 'learning ladder' on the PC, watching DVDs, etc., while I develop training outlines and lesson plans. In fact, I did a lot of this while finishing off this book to enable me to meet certain deadlines.

The need for balance isn't just about our children and husband; it's about us as individuals too. We are tri-part beings, meaning we are made up of body, soul and spirit. You *are* a spirit, you *have* a soul, and you *live* in a body. This means that we have a responsibility to take care of our whole being. Eating and drinking well, getting enough rest and me-time, meeting up with friends, wearing nice things, etc., are all actions we can take to look after our body.

Soul care is all about feeding our soul with healthy information by what we read, watch, or listen to. No wonder the Bible says it is what comes from inside that defiles us.

> Mark 7:20-23
> *He went on: "What comes out of a person is what defiles them. For it is from within, out of a person's heart, that evil thoughts come—sexual immorality, theft, murder, adultery, greed, malice, deceit, lewdness, envy, slander, arrogance and folly. All these evils come from inside and defile a person."*

Just as eating junk food has a negative impact on our health, junk information destroys our soul. As a very young girl, I was exposed to books with lots of sexual content which made my imagination go wild and introduced a lot of spiritual baggage into my life. What you imagine, think, say and do come out of what you've allowed into your heart through reading, listening, hearing and watching. As you re-launch your career, you need to develop the habit of disallowing negative things from entering into your soul. So, for example, when you are asked to join in the gossip ring at work, be quick to politely decline.

Our spirit is God's nature in us, so to take care of our spirit we need to spend time with God and allow Him to refresh us. In our busyness it's very easy to carry on for days without spending time with Him. When I get easily frustrated or start getting completely overwhelmed by challenges, I know that I have neglected spending time with God. I was not as organised as I am now, and in the past my children would still be awake at 9:45 pm, which meant I couldn't really get some me-time. Now they go to bed between 7:30 and 7:45 pm, which then gives me time for my daily devotion and other things. I once attended a conference where one of the speakers talked about using a daily management plan, which is simply writing down everything one wants to do when one wakes up every morning. I must confess that I have not fully embraced this concept. However, the few times I have done so, it really worked; I found it easy to focus and achieve the things on my list. It also made it easy for me not to take on things which I had not set out to do that particular day.

Money, money, money

Money can be a potential roadblock for many re-launchers. Whilst I cannot give any concrete financial advice, I have included some tips below and included details of organisations which may be able to offer you some help at the end of this book. Understanding your present situation will enable you to make decisions about your return to the workplace. To be in a good position to make these decisions, you need to know what your monthly outgoings are, as well as how much you need to earn to cover these costs.

Throughout my re-launch journey, God has always showed up, even if at the last minute. I even started joking that God likes doing things at the last minute! He is truly a God of provision. Here are a few tips that may help:

DON'T STOP GIVING

This is a biblical principle and is covered in more detail in the next chapter.

TAKE A FREE MONEY HEALTH CHECK ONLINE

You can do this at:
https://healthcheck.moneyadviceservice.org.uk/

TAKE UP THE CHALLENGE OF MONEY MANAGEMENT

Attitude is crucial. If you're married, talk it over with your husband. Try to reach consensus concerning the importance of cutting back. This is crucial because your success may require some sacrifice and that means cooperation from other members of your family.

STICK TO A BUDGET

How can you know where your money is going if you don't budget? How can you set spending and saving goals if you don't know where your money is going? Set up a simple and practical budget that enables you to manage your expenses each month.

PAY OFF CREDIT CARD DEBT

Credit card debt is the number one obstacle to getting ahead financially. Those little pieces of plastic are so easy to use, and it's easy to forget that it's real money we're dealing with when we use them to pay for purchases. Despite our good desires to pay the balance off quickly, the reality is that we often don't, and we end up paying far more for things than we would have paid if we had used cash.

REVIEW YOUR INSURANCE COVERAGE

Too many people are talked into paying too much for life, home and car insurance. Some buy whole-life insurance policies when term-life makes more sense, or life insurance when they have no dependents. Try shopping around to see if you can get a better deal. When I originally went on maternity leave, my husband and I reviewed all our expenses; we switched our utility and insurance providers and got rid of our cable TV services.

INVEST WISELY AND UPDATE YOUR WILL

When you start working, you will benefit from speaking to a financial advisor to explore your options. If you have dependents, no matter how little or how much you own, you need a will.

KEEP GOOD RECORDS

If you don't keep good records, you'll find it difficult to claim all your allowable income tax deductions and credits. Whether you are self-employed or own your own business, setting up a system will make it easier for you, instead of you scrambling to find everything when you need to complete your tax returns.

DISTINGUISH BETWEEN WANTS AND NEEDS

Every time you want to buy something, ask yourself if you really need the item.

PRACTICE PRUDENCE

Find ways to have fun without spending money: a day at the park versus shopping at the mall, a film night with popcorn in your home versus going to the cinema. Don't be afraid to shop around for the best price. There are lots of discount vouchers available online.

Claudine's story

Claudine re-launched her career as a businesswoman, but with greater clarity and renewed focus, after a one-year break.

As a business owner, I am not really sure if you can have a business break. Even when I am not 'physically' at work, my mind is always thinking about the future.

I did however take a break away from my business after the birth of my second child. I took time out (twelve months) to pursue another area of interest. This period actually turned into a period of self-discovery, and I came out stronger, wiser and better able to be more effective in my business. After my career break, I was able to start from a difference place mentally, emotionally and with a stronger strategic vision.

My husband and I have always worked together; he has been my greatest supporter. I am blessed to have a wonderful family who, when necessary, have always helped with childcare (which will be the concern of most women in business).

In re-launching my career, my main challenge was overcoming self-sabotaging, toxic thoughts that were accompanied with self-doubt and a lack of belief in the gifts God had deposited in me. Once I was able to re-position my mind and become focused, I was able to walk in purpose.

My advice to women planning to re-launch their career would be that they focus on balancing the key areas of their lives: faith, family, fitness, and finance. Given that under the sun we are all equal and all have twenty-four hours, the important question is, how do you organise your time?

Faith *is all about being connected with God, spending time in prayer and meditation to draw strength, wisdom, confidence and direction.*

Family*. Ensure you make time for family; at the end of the day they matter the most. A woman on her dying bed has never said, "I wish I spent more time at the office."*

Fitness *refers not only to the physical but also takes into account mental, emotional and spiritual.*

Finance *refers to the finance-savvy woman that is able to leave instant gratification for longer term financial success.*

Do you have staying power?

Knowing what you want to achieve in your career or business is great, but the real question is, do you have staying power? What do you do if you don't succeed right away? Do you give up or do you keep working at it? History books contain records of men and women who overcame adversity by not allowing failure, obstacles, disappointments, etc. to stop them from fulfilling their dreams. If we trust God and focus on moving forward, we will be creating alternatives and possibilities for ourselves and those around us.

> *Unless God has raised you up for this very thing, you will be worn out by the opposition of men and devils. But if*

God be for you, who can be against you? Are all of them together stronger than God? O be not weary of well doing!

– John Wesley

What about when work's not working?

What if, after all your efforts, you land a job only to discover that the environment is toxic or that your boss is a nightmare? I had a tough time when I returned to work after the birth of my daughter. I dreaded going to work every day. My line manager made life difficult for me. I did not allow God to shine through me in that situation; instead I joined in the gossip and deliberately ignored my manager. The fact is she made life unbearable for me, as she did for others, but I should have related to her as a child of God. I am not advocating that we become doormats or put ourselves in harm's way, but in my particular situation the Holy Spirit tried to help me respond in love – but I was too annoyed to even listen. I have discovered that in order to prune us and work on our character, God sometimes allows us to go through certain painful experiences. I often wonder at how David was able to keep playing the harp knowing fully well that Saul was trying to kill him. Even after Saul made more attempts on his life, David chose not to take matters into his own hands and instead asked God to intervene. This ultimately led to his promotion. As you re-launch your career, do bear it in mind that the first job you get may well be a stepping stone or bridge to the place God has prepared for you.

If you end up in a career and then realise that it's not really for you, always remember that it is never too late to refresh, regroup and re-launch again.

Suzanne's story

Suzanne works as a shop manager and re-launched her career after a four-year break.

I gave up work when my first baby was born, and was a stay-at-home mum for four years until the breakdown of my marriage. This was a really traumatic time for all of us, but God was constant through it all. He was, and is, the only person I could depend on. Although I had been a Christian for over twenty years, it was at this time that I discovered God is faithful and trustworthy, He is a strong tower and a shield; I finally understood a bit of what He meant when He said in the Bible that His name is 'I am' – He is my everything. I had a few part-time jobs at this time, earning the bare minimum I was allowed on income support, and learned that God is my provider. He taught me to tithe, and although at the time I couldn't imagine being able to afford to tithe, once I started to faithfully and cheerfully give to God, I discovered His miraculous provision. It really is true that if you give God 10% of your income He blesses the 90% you have left. I learnt to claim and speak out scriptures for provision and protection, Psalm 91 being one that I pray every day, and my house became a house of prayer and praise. It was a struggle managing on such a small amount of income, but God showed me how, and we never went without. We had amazing provision of food and clothing and saw God really come through for us when we stood in faith, believing Him for the things we needed.

In the months before my youngest child started school, I started looking for a new job. I tried to get jobs in schools so that I could have the holidays off but this didn't happen. Then I applied for a job in an office; there were lots of applicants but amazingly none of them except for me returned their completed application forms on time, and I was offered the job at my interview. I was so grateful to be in work and completely ignored the things that were wrong. I was treated badly by my boss but was really scared that if I spoke up I would lose my job and have to go back on income support or be without money for a while. This would mean having nowhere to live and losing everything so I put up with it all and never spoke out. In fairness to my employer, I don't think she had an idea how unfair she was being and was just really happy to have such a compliant employee. However it all came to a head one day when she found out I had applied for another job. During this time God spoke to me about acting with integrity and doing everything in love – I did this with His strength, although there were a lot of tears and phone calls to the Citizens Advice Bureau and ACAS. Interestingly I didn't get the other job, but God miraculously opened up another door for me and gave me such peace I knew that was the path I was meant to take, even though it was not what I had had in mind for my life. I have never enjoyed working anywhere as much as I do now!

I gained confidence through starting the first job – it showed me I was employable. I had had good, well-paid jobs before I had the children, but being a stay-at-home mum and being in an abusive and toxic marriage had left me feeling insecure and completely devoid of confidence in my abilities, so I am grateful for that job. I believe it was the stepping stone I needed to then go into my present role with the confidence to know I could do it well.

There are still ongoing financial issues, but I know for sure who my Provider is, and I am able to stand more in faith now when the problems come. I found putting my children with a childminder really hard too – it wasn't something I ever thought I would have to do and I felt really guilty – but they are fine. They don't look forward to the childminder days because they prefer being with me, but they are always okay and they are safe. They understand that they need to be there when I work. I struggled with being a working mum and felt I was letting my children down, but God showed me the image of the godly wife in the book of Proverbs, and to my complete amazement she was a working mum!

Our house isn't perfect – it's very often a complete mess – but for now this is okay. We have a plaque up on our wall which says, "In this house we do real, we do I'm sorry, we do fun, we do hugs, we do really loud, we do second chances, we do happy, we do forgiveness, we do love," and that sums us up – we do our best and we do love. Although my life isn't the way I thought it would be, we are happy. I have a job which I really enjoy, two beautiful children, and a heavenly Father who helps me to be their mum and gives me strength, wisdom and guidance. I have a wonderful Saviour and Redeemer and an amazing Comforter who is leading me into all truth.

If I had to name three things I needed to successfully re-launch my career, at the top would be God; He is my all in all. Second would be good childcare in place, knowing my children are safe and well-cared for. And thirdly would be the support of family and a friend who helped me with a great CV (thank you, Veronica) as well as advice and support whenever I needed it.

Questions for reflections:

What challenges are you facing right now?

_____

_____

_____

_____

_____

How do these challenges measure against God?

_____

_____

_____

_____

How can you develop staying power?

_____

_____

_____

_____

CHAPTER ELEVEN

Let Your Light Shine

What is the point of having a successful career that doesn't bring glory to God? This is a question we need to ask ourselves often. My desire is that my career pursuits will bring glory to God and transform those around me.

The book of Acts contains numerous examples of supernatural events that occurred in the marketplace. We also should expect and pray for similar occurrences in our organisations, communities, schools, businesses, etc. We need to have an understanding that we are worshiping God through our careers.

If every time a teacher teaches, a baker bakes a cake, a trainer trains a group of people, a cleaner cleans the toilets or a shopkeeper attends to customers, we do it in honour and worship of God, I am convinced that more lives will be transformed and we will see God's Kingdom come in our workplaces.

Whilst working on a recent consulting project, I had several opportunities to meet and speak to three women at different times. These women included the HR Director who had head-hunted me, my direct line manager and the partnership manager responsible for monitoring the work carried out by all associates. I believe God placed these women in my path for specific reasons. During conversations with them, they would often make statements such as:

- "You are a force for good."
- "There's a light about you."
- "You always brighten the room when you come in."
- "You are an inspiration and good motivator for others."

I felt deeply humbled by these statements and it dawned on me that as children of God we are lights. This means that wherever we work our lights should shine brightly. It is a real honour to be able to represent our loving Father in this way. In all honesty, I never thought of my life in this vein until I gave up my job in 2011. I am not proud of the way I presented myself in some previous roles – I was resentful and was always keen to join in office gossip about the bad practice by some senior managers. Now I know better, and one of my prayers whenever I start a new project is that God would help me to portray Him in the right way and that I would be a blessing to at least one person. Looking back, God has been faithful in answering this prayer.

Blessed to be a blessing

Part of lighting up our sphere of influence includes raising and building up others too. As I mentioned before, when I started supporting women I was passionate but didn't really have compassion. It took God's intervention to show me that even though I was running workshops for women, I did not really care about them. In His faithfulness, He has taught me to give to others even when it's not convenient. We can give time, money, gifts, an encouraging word, etc. Sometimes we are so engrossed in organising large conferences, thinking that this is the most effective way to reach out to others. But the truth is there are so many people around us that we can bless. Often we fail to see them in our misplaced zeal to do something big for God.

This was brought home to me by my own personal experience of working with lone parents on benefits, many of whom are going through much pain and difficulty. There are so many people in our churches, workplaces, communities and families who are going to bed hungry, dying of loneliness and begging for someone to reach out to them. I wrote this book in the midst of a terrible 'storm', and I cannot tell you the number of days and nights that I hoped that someone would bring me a bowl of cooked food! This is not because I had no food; rather I found that because of the challenges cooking was usually one of the last things on my mind. Don't get me wrong; I did manage to cook sometimes because I have the responsibility to do so (especially as a mother to two young children) but at other times I relied on ordering cooked food or takeaways.

I have shared this to ignite something in your heart and to challenge you as you step out into the marketplace. I am truly hoping that as you go forth, you will ask God to open your eyes to opportunities around you where you can be a real blessing. I am praying that as we re-launch our careers we will extend a hand of friendship and fellowship to other women around us who need support to do the same too.

I want to quickly mention about tithing. The word 'tithe' means tenth or 10%. A tithe is the first 10% of your income. The Bible says the purpose of tithing is to teach us always to put God first in our lives. Tithing is a reminder that God is the supplier of everything we have. It is also God's personal invitation to an outpouring of His blessing in our lives.

In Malachi, God says this:

Malachi 3:10 (NLT)
"Bring the whole tithe into the storehouse, that there may be food in my house. Test me in this," says the LORD Almighty, "and see if I will not throw open the floodgates of heaven and pour out so much blessing that there will not be room enough to store it."

This is the only place in scripture where God tells us to put Him to the test. In other words, he's saying, "Go ahead. I dare you. See if you can out-give me."

The Bible has certain principles which, when applied, yield remarkable results. For years, I did not pay my tithes consistently. I only paid them after settling all necessary bills. Sometimes I would borrow money from my tithe with the plan of returning it, but of course I rarely did. Interestingly no one convinced me to reassess my ways. The Holy Spirit taught me Himself, not in a forceful way but in a gentle and loving way. How God must love me and how foolish I have been! Now I pay my tithes monthly and God has been so faithful. Sometimes I still get tempted to borrow from it, but I made a decision that regardless of the expenses I need to make every month, my tithe must be the first thing to leave my account. I believe that any organisation or business set up based on kingdom principles will benefit from tithing too.

If you trust God then you should trust Him with all aspects of your life, including your finances. Start tithing faithfully and watch what He does in and through your life

The little foxes

A friend of mine agreed that I could share this story. My friend was working on a project at work, and as part of this she had to sort out boxes of children's toys and products. Whilst sorting through the products, the temptation to take one of the toys for her son was so strong that she succumbed to it. She took a toy and quickly kept it in her bag before anyone saw her. A few minutes later she heard the gentle voice of the Holy Spirit telling her she had stolen something that did not belong to her. She felt ashamed and very quickly returned the toy to the box. She said she felt it was okay to take the toy especially because there were loads of them and the toys were actually going to be donated to charities and individuals. Furthermore her son had asked her for a toy on the previous day. However, the Holy Spirit made it clear that what she had done was wrong and unacceptable. Not long after she returned the toy, one of the coordinators came in and said, "Oh, please feel free to take some of the toys for your boys." You can imagine how she felt. She explained that she had struggled with taking things that did not belong to her from a very young age and had been asking the Holy Spirit to help her overcome this problem. And He sure did! I used to take things that did not belong to me when I was much younger, and I remember how much I struggled with this vice. It was a battle which I won through the help of the Holy Spirit.

I have shared this story to draw our attention to the things that we do in the workplace and discard as normal. I have heard cases of cleaners who steal toilet rolls and hand gels. I once heard the story of a lady who would remove used stamps from letters at work for her personal use later.

Or how about when we cheat on our hours or sneak out to do our personal shopping during work time? Many people do not consider these things to be sin, but sin is sin and God has clear standards. I recently heard about the renowned head teacher who had secretly been using school funds for personal interests.

Whatever job we do, it will help us to do it as though we are doing it unto the Lord. God is not mocked, and He sees what we do in secret even when no one else does. What would happen if God chose to visit our workplaces in human form, just like on the popular TV series Undercover Boss?

Give up your job

What do you think? You've just landed a great job or started a new business or community project – am I now suggesting that you give it all up? Yes, that's right, but it's not what you think! I mean, give up your job to God and place it in His hands as a sacrifice.

Before I re-launched as a consultant, I went through a phase where the Holy Spirit showed me what it means to be a true worshipper. A true worshipper is a person whose heart is devoted to God and who does not hold anything back to honour God. A true worshipper will gladly give her job or business to God because she understands that it is not hers in the first place. I remember begging God that I never want to become too engrossed in my work or business pursuits and that I want Him to always be first in my life.

As working women we will go through different situations and tests which will reveal where our hearts really lie. If our primary reason for working is to amass wealth then we've got it all wrong. Jesus said:

> Matthew 6:19-21
> *Do not store up for yourselves treasures on earth, where moths and vermin destroy, and where thieves break in and steal. But store up for yourselves treasures in heaven, where moths and vermin do not destroy, and where thieves do not break in and steal. For where your treasure is, there your heart will be also.*

Let me give you an example which you can relate to. I decided to get involved in a monthly lunchtime outreach to express God's love to stay-at-home mums and other women in a particular community. Not long after I committed to doing this, I was offered some training delivery opportunities. I needed the money so this was great news. However, one of the dates was on the same date as our proposed outreach. As my training contact read out the dates, I did a quick calculation of how much I would lose by rejecting to deliver the training session. It was so tempting – but I quickly declined and explained that I had another appointment on that particular day.

William McDowell's song, 'I give myself away', says it all. Our main goal is to live for God and pursue Him. In other words, there is nothing more important in life than to love God, please Him, know Him, serve Him, spend time with Him and make Him our heart's desire and treasure. Everything else should come after.

Questions for reflection

What are the little foxes in your life?

_____

_____

_____

_____

Give examples of how you can shine for Christ in your workplace or community.

_____

_____

_____

_____

_____

_____

Chapter Twelve

Lessons by Doing

Many people never make changes or do things differently because they are scared of failure or losing the things they have. What they don't realise is that they lose so much more by not stepping out. Below are some of the general lessons I learnt by doing.

Think like an entrepreneur

I have heard many people say this, and it is true. To successfully re-launch your career, you need to think like an entrepreneur. And I don't mean this as a cliché. This applies to you even if you are not thinking of setting up a business. Your skills are your product, your potential employers are your customers, and your salary is your income. Passionate, risk-taker, efficient and unconventional are some of the characteristics of entrepreneurs. So go ahead, think like an entrepreneur and get your career moving!

Decide on your core values

Before I set up my business I decided on some core values which have helped me all the way through. Not only do values help in giving focus, they also ensure that I don't compromise on my faith and ethos. My values influence the way I relate to my clients and the associate trainers who work for my organisation. One of my core values is compassion, and this has an impact on all the areas of my business. For example, I always ensure that associate trainers are paid on time. My rationale is that as they are self-employed, being paid on time will help them with cash flow. When delivering training sessions,

I use exercises and tools which are inclusive and respond to the individual needs of learners. When coaching women looking to re-launch their careers, I am driven by my compassion to see them break out into their dreams and purposes.

Jack of all trades, yet master of all

My first taste of business showed me that one can juggle different roles and achieve good results, even if for a short period of time. I say a short period of time because as the business grows a solid team will be required to take the business to greater heights. When I was on maternity leave, following the birth of my son, I decided to test the waters and host my first career development and recruitment event for women. This is probably one of the most daunting things I have ever done. I was a one-woman band with no real savings and no key contacts. One thing I had was the ability to carry out good research using the Internet, and I made best use of this.

Out-think your size

From my little bedroom, saddled with my six-month-old son, I started researching about other local, national and international women-focused recruitment events. I wanted to create a national event that would open up opportunities for skilled women. This was no easy task, but once I had my husband's support I set out to work. The Internet, social media and strategic network alliances have undoubtedly opened up the world, which means that you can extend your reach and work wonders from your bedroom, shed, garage or kitchen. The Internet helped me to stop thinking local and made me step up to explore national opportunities. With the World Wide Web, really the world's our oyster.

Marketing without a budget

I recently read the story of Julie Deane, who founded Cambridge Satchel Company in her kitchen in 2008 with £600. After working tirelessly to develop her products, Julie Deane put herself on every free online listing she knew of — from the Yellow Pages to eBay to mom blogs. She saw the Internet as a tool to her success, and she maximised it.

As a one-woman show, I developed a business plan and identified some of the key roles required for this project. My list included sales and marketing, customer service, copywriting, administration, etc. I got an organisation to develop a website and wrote all the required content. I approached various organisations for partnerships and sponsorships, and successfully got organisations such as The Pensions Advisory Service, Real World Publications, TM Lewin, etc. to support the event. TM Lewin provided shirts and also supported the event with their presence. Real World featured the event in their Diversity Magazine which is distributed at various universities. In return, I offered them a stand each at the event and promised to feature them on the event website. I even managed to get Body Shop products for all delegates courtesy of one of their Area Leaders. I learnt something vital, which is that many people are ready to help if approached. None of the speakers charged me; instead I offered them various opportunities from featuring them on the website, allowing them to sell their books at the event, etc. The calibre of speakers helped boost the credibility of the event greatly.

I remember emailing and making calls directly to HR Directors, to tell them about the event and invite their organisation to exhibit for a fee. Before making each call, I would literally sweat and breathe in several times. I would lock myself up in the wardrobe to drain out any background noise. I didn't want them to hear the cooing of my baby. Once they responded, I would then email them as a member of the sales team, using my company's second email address. I managed to get organisations such as Allianz, Enterprise Rent-A-Car, London Fire Brigade, Metropolitan Police, Marston Group, etc. to exhibit at this pilot event. Our leaflet distributing service was made up of my husband and me. After generating a list of different women organisations, academic institutions, groups, etc., we sent off promotional flyers attached to a letter of invitation. A number of these organisations welcomed the invitations and helped us promote the event. I also made use of free event listings as best as I could.

Perfect one craft right and then fly

For women who want to re-launch as portfolio workers, I suggest that you decide on one or two things to master before springing off to do other things. In my own case, I initially developed my competence and skills in the field of Learning and Organisational Development, and later focused on enhancing my skills as a Trainer, with a specific focus on career development and soft skills. This has served as a good fall-back cushion or safety net, making it easy for me to switch lanes when work is not coming through in one area. I believe that everything has a season – there is time to build up one's reputation in one area, and there's a season to branch off into other things. But please do not believe the popular opinion that you need to focus on just one area. Whatever your mind can conceive, you can achieve. It's okay to break the rules and soar.

Value your time

How many times have you agreed to do something for free and then bitten your lip in frustration and regret? I give God all the glory for blessing me with some really good skills, one of which is CV writing. People ask me how I am able to churn out so many CVs in a short period of time. But there was a time when this skill became an inundating task. I stopped enjoying it, primarily because people started taking advantage of my skill and niceness, knowingly and unknowingly. It wasn't uncommon to receive emails from close friends, asking me to kindly have a look at their CV and suggest how they can improve it. Some asked outright for my help in developing new CVs; others would ask for the cost of writing a CV and then give me stories about money being tight.

Please don't get me wrong; I have happily written CVs and supported people in completing application forms without feeling bad, because many of them were going through tough times and genuinely could not afford to pay. However, about a year and a half ago, I realised that CV writing was part of my business and not a charity. I was not making the best use of my time. On average it takes two to three hours to write a good CV. So imagine that my hourly rate is £80 per hour; that's three hours and £240 gone forever. I guess you could say it wouldn't be so bad if some of the people asking for favours could not afford to pay. The reality is most of them *can* afford to pay but simply don't value my time or their career development enough to make that investment. No one would go to the supermarket and ask for free supplies. At the end of the day a business is a business and you need to make purposeful profit.

Know your worth, name your fee

For a long time, I didn't know my worth and suffered as a result. I was once head-hunted by an HR Director of a public sector organisation. After a brief chat, she asked, "What's your daily rate?" I was not prepared and gave her a figure for a four-hour role which I had just completed. This was a big mistake as the role I was being head-hunted for was a 7.2-hour role. I eventually went back to her to renegotiate my fee. The business books say this isn't very professional, but in this case I had no choice. Like Nehemiah, I shot an arrow of prayer to heaven, refreshed my knowledge on having crucial conversations and told her what I had done wrong. Fortunately, she agreed to an increase in my daily rate. It's a mistake I will never make again.

Here are a few tips that may help:

- *Value the investment in yourself.*
  Try not to do things for nothing. However, there are times when the Holy Spirit will prompt you to help. When this happens, please do help, as this will lead to more blessings for you.
- *Always be prepared to name your fee.*
  When you are paid well, you can work more effectively.
- *Always include the time for preparation.*
- *Name your real fee and don't apologise.*
  Regardless of what the media says about the economy, base your fee on your investments and proposed work output.
- *Learn to negotiate.*
  Don't just accept what people offer you.

My 5 E Model

I developed this approach for a presentation on 'Succeeding as a black and minority ethnic individual in the British marketplace'. It's relevant to anyone who wants to develop a successful career, whether as an employee or business owner. Here's a summary of the model:

EXCELLENCE

Every individual or organisation needs to have a framework in place which supports the execution of tasks and realisation of goals. From providing good customer service, maintaining a professional approach, to keeping good records, a lot of processes can be implemented to ensure excellence. As a child of God, this is very important for us. I frown when people tell me one cannot do business without cutting corners. I once had a discussion with a Christian gentleman who tried to rationalise why it is okay to adopt certain practices in the workplace. Personally, I'd rather be ethical and act with integrity than run a business on a faulty foundation. Let's make no mistake; our God is a Master of Excellence.

EXPOSURE

Regardless of where you are operating, it is vital that you understand the culture and focus on networking and developing key relationships that will support the achievement of your business and career goals. I have an informal advisory board made up of people from different walks of life. I contact these individuals as and when the need arises. Who are the key people in your life, and what roles do they play?

EXPRESSION

Whether returning to the workplace or setting up a business, it is important that we are able to express ourselves. We cannot hide from this. Interviews, giving presentations, pitching products and net-working are all examples of situations where we need to be able to communicate our brand. As a trainer and motivational speaker, this is an area that I must definitely continue to work on. Thankfully there are many ways to develop our expression; individuals can join Toastmasters to develop their public speaking skills, take courses on elocution and branding, get a CV expert to work on their CV or refresh their business' marketing strategy.

EXPLORATION

Recreate or die. Have you heard this term before? I believe we need to continuously carry out research to expand our knowledge and horizon so that we can stay relevant. Those who are in the field of consulting will tell you how useful it is to research. I learnt very quickly that when asked to do something by a client it is okay to say, "I will get back to you with more information (or a proposition) shortly." This gives one time to research and develop something that could potentially wow the client. Every individual or business has a lifecycle; keep thinking forward and introducing new ideas.

EVALUATION

Performance management isn't just for big organisations; it's for every forward-thinking individual. I enjoy receiving feedback from my clients as this helps me to make key improvements and reinvent myself so I can access different markets.

My top lessons

I have learnt so many lessons in my 're-launch journey', but without a doubt these are my biggest ones:

TRUSTING GOD

I know without a doubt that my strength, intelligence, qualifications and connections can only take me so far. I once read that a thousand days' hard work cannot give what a minute's favour will give one. Nothing can compare with God's favour. God continues to amaze me by opening doors and providing me with opportunities that I could only dream of. This is why I always stress that whilst tools and plans are great, they are definitely not self-sufficient.

KNOWING GOD

Having a mission statement or vision statement without an 'intimacy statement' will cause us to burn out. We must continue to spend time in God's presence to know Him more and listen for His wisdom in all things.

PRAYER

Every good thing that makes a lasting and divine difference is born out of prayer. This has probably been the biggest lesson of all for me. Prayer unlocks doors; it brings revelation; it gives direction; it gives succour in tough times.

LETTING GO AND LETTING GOD

I remain indebted to my heavenly Father for taking me on a tough and painful journey where I had to lose many things in order to truly understand that, as John 12:24 says, "...unless a grain of wheat falls into the ground and dies, it remains alone; but if it dies, it produces much grain".

PATIENCE AND PERSISTENCE:

No career plan ever becomes reality as quickly as we want; neither does any business ever grow as quickly as we want. No business is ever as profitable as soon as we'd like. It takes quite a while for one to build one's credibility and professional reputation. So we need tons and tons of patience and resilience.

FAILURE AND REJECTION

Failure presents us with the opportunity to start again. I felt discouraged and closed my first business after making a loss. I have come against several obstacles and rejections in my life. The truth is there will always be obstacles, and when you come up against them you have a choice: give up or find a way around them. Instead of saying, "I can't," you have to say, "Lord, help make this happen; show me how I can make this happen." Then you have to take action to do what needs to be done. No excuses!

STEPPING OUT IN FAITH

It is perfectly okay to be unreasonable. By this I mean doing something which you believe God has impressed in your heart to do but which is guaranteed to attract people's cynicism and discouraging comments. When God spoke to Abraham the first time, He told him to leave his father's house to go to a place that He would show him. Abraham didn't know where he was going; he only knew where he couldn't stay. Can you imagine how Abraham must have felt inside? I am sure he had his moments of fear and doubts, but he chose to step out in faith and serves as a good model for us.

TALENTS AND GIFTS

To whom much is given, much is expected. Talents and gifts in themselves are never enough. They come with great responsibility. We need the right attitude and character. Above all it is sobering to know that we will give an account of what we do with the things which God has given us.

RELATIONSHIPS

Isolation is the dream-killer. We all need to surround ourselves with trusted people. It may just be one or two people that we can be open and honest with. Tell them what you're struggling with. Asking for help doesn't make us wimps!

PRIORITIES

My main priority must be to live for Christ. This means all that I am and all that I do should reflect Him at all times. I also have a responsibility to bring my children up in a way that will make them reflect Christ. I understand that God appointed me as a custodian for His precious jewels; hence my role as a mother must not be taken lightly.

Questions for reflection

What are your core values?

_____

_____

_____

_____

Can you list some of the little things which you particularly want to avoid doing after you re-launch your career?

_____

_____

_____

_____

What particular lessons apply to you?

_____

_____

_____

_____

Prayer Nuggets

GIVING

Ask God to help you become a giver. Tell Him to work on your heart.

PROVISION

Pray that God will pour out His abundance on you and your family. Pray that lack will be a thing of the past in your home.

VICTORY

Ask God to give you victory over the challenges that are threatening your re-launch plans. Pray that the overcoming power of Christ will be activated in your life.

CHARACTER

Ask God to help you build a godly character. Pray that God's powerful light will flush out the 'little foxes'[12] in your life.

---

[12] Songs of Solomon 2:15

Reflective Exercises for Part I: Get Up

Activity 1: Confidence

The following statements reflect important information regarding how you may be feeling about yourself. Be honest and tick the ones that apply to you. Please note that this quiz is not a formal measure of confidence.

Tick one item per row that applies to you.

Group A	Group B
☐ I expect to succeed in performing important tasks	☐ I expect to fail in performing important tasks
☐ I am as important as other colleagues even though I have been away from work for a while.	☐ I am less important than other colleagues because I have been away from work for a while
☐ It is easy to express my feelings and thoughts	☐ I have difficulty with expressing my feelings and thoughts
☐ It is easy to have conversations with new people	☐ It is difficult to have conversations with new people
☐ I am as intelligent as most people	☐ I am less intelligent than most people
☐ I think that most people I know like me	☐ I think that most people I know don't like me
☐ I do not easily feel depressed	☐ I easily feel depressed
☐ I am as good looking as most	☐ I am not as good looking as most
☐ I am usually relaxed and at ease with myself	☐ I am usually tense or anxious
☐ My feelings are not easily hurt	☐ My feelings are easily hurt
☐ I am not more sensitive than most	☐ I am more sensitive than most
☐ I do not worry a lot	☐ I worry a lot

☐ I enjoy receiving compliments

☐ I feel uneasy receiving compliments

☐ I enjoy complimenting others on their accomplishments

☐ I don't compliment others

Write your total number of ticks for Group A: _____

Write your total number of ticks for Group B: _____

Think about the result. What picture do your answers depict? What story do they tell? Write or draw this below:

Get up, Create, Break out

What makes you feel confident?

_____

_____

_____

_____

What makes you less confident?

_____

_____

_____

_____

What can you do to increase your confidence?

_____

_____

_____

_____

Activity 2: Your identity – who are you?

WHO AM I? OUTER IDENTITY

Your outer identity is developed as you grow up and relate to particular people around you. For example:

- You identify yourself as 'British' because you are a citizen.
- When you get married you are known as a 'wife'.
- When you have children you are known as a 'mum'.
- If you sing in the church choir you become a 'choir member'.

Complete this mind map with phrases/words that describe how you identify yourself.

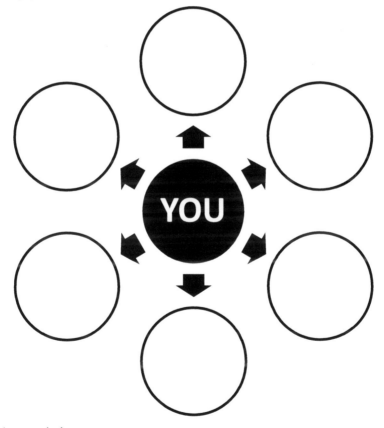

Add more below:

Get up, Create, Break out

WHO AM I? INNER IDENTITY

Your inner identity is more subtle and not obvious; it is about the way you feel, what you think, what you say and how you act. It's about your personality, cultural background, feelings and thoughts about yourself, your emotional responses to life and how you respond and deal with other people as well as situations and challenges, etc.

Complete this mind map with phrases/words that describe how you identify yourself.

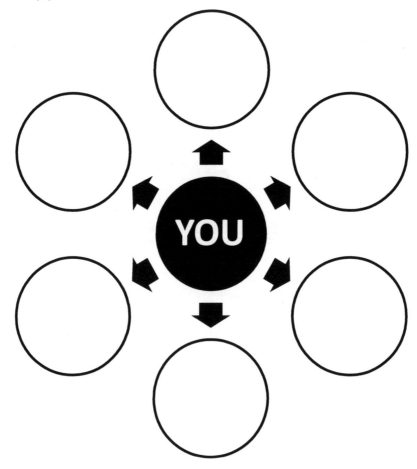

Add more below:

Let's explore how the following people have influenced your identity:

	What they said (or say)	How this made/makes you feel
Parents		
Siblings		
Husband		
Teachers		
Colleagues/ Boss		
Friends		

Get up, Create, Break out

Now let's look at who *God* says you really are (search the Bible for scriptures that describe who you are).

The Bible says (verse)	What does this mean?	How does this make you feel?

Activity 3: Your aspirations, achievements and goals

What are your aspirations?

_____

_____

_____

What are your fears and concerns?

_____

_____

_____

List five of your achievements below:

1.
_____
2.
_____
3.
_____
4.
_____
5.
_____

Who/what helped you attain these achievements?

_____

_____

Get up, Create, Break out

List your goals below:

Short-term goals

_____

_____

_____

_____

_____

_____

_____

Long-term goals

_____

_____

_____

_____

_____

_____

_____

Reflective Exercises for Part II: Create

Activity 1: Career considerations

How do you feel?

_____

_____

_____

What support network have you identified to help you?

_____

_____

How many hours do you want to work?

_____

Do you want to work part time or full time?

_____

Do you want to go back to work part-time and then gradually build up to full-time?

_____

Get up, Create, Break out

What working pattern will suit you (days, evenings, nights)?

_____

_____

How far can you travel for work?

_____

How much money do you need to earn to make working worthwhile for you?

_____

What are your childcare options?

_____

_____

Have you factored childcare costs into your salary?

_____

What skills do you need to brush up on first?

_____

_____

_____

What are the latest tools and equipment used in your sector?

_____

_____

Which of these tools and equipment (if any) do you need to learn to use?

_____

What training programmes can you do?

_____

_____

Do you want to set up your own business?

_____

What business idea (if any) do you have?

_____

_____

What research have you carried out about this idea?

_____

_____

What have you said to your husband and children about your re-launch plans?

_____

_____

What contingency plans do you have in place should things go wrong?

_____

_____

Activity 2: Identifying your support network

What do you feel you are able to do alone?

_____

_____

_____

What do you think you'll need help with?

_____

_____

_____

Try to think of different people or places in your current network, that can help you with your re-launch plan.

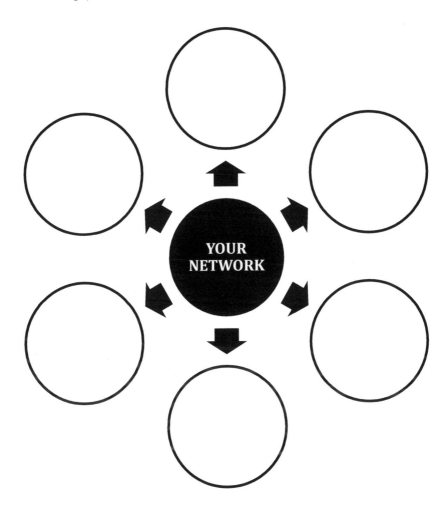

What help do you need that is not available in your existing network? How can you access this help?

_____

_____

Activity 3: CV Building – What you've got going for you

List the fields you think you would like to go into. If you have a clear idea about what you want to do in the future, that's great. Even if you don't, you can still have a good CV.

_____

_____

_____

List all the work you have ever done. It does not matter whether you did not earn money doing this work.

_____

_____

_____

_____

_____

List any organisations you have belonged to.

_____

_____

_____

_____

_____

List any personal development or refresher courses you have taken.

_____

_____

_____

List all the voluntary work you have ever done for your church, children's school, neighbours, and friends. What are the things you found yourself doing again and again during your career break?

_____

_____

_____

List your favourite interests.

_____

_____

_____

List your strengths. Are you good at motivating others? Are you good at organising events?

_____

_____

_____

Reflective Exercises for Part III: Break Out

Activity 1a: Roadblocks / mountains

A number of things can get in the way of your re-launch plan, some of which can totally destroy your plan while others might distract you from your main objectives. Knowing what your personal re-launch roadblocks are will ensure that you are well prepared to sweep them to one side.

If your husband does not support your plans, what can you do?

_____

_____

_____

If you lack investment money, what can you do?

_____

_____

_____

What other potential roadblocks are there?

_____

_____

_____

What can you do about them?

_____

_____

_____

_____

Activity 1b: Money

List the different ways in which you can:

1. Cut back on your expenditure

_____

_____

_____

_____

2. Raise funds to support your re-launch plan

_____

_____

_____

_____

A Quick 'How To' Guide for your Re-launch Action Plan

Congratulations! If you are on this page, it means you have read through the three sections of this book. To leave the dreaming and thinking stage, you now need to take action. Your action plan is meant to be a simple tool to help you on your way. The action plan provided is an eight-month plan.

Points to consider carefully

- *Read through the whole book, if you haven't done so already.*
  Feel free to doodle, think creatively, make notes, underline or highlight important and relevant points using a highlighter.

- *Allocate time to study the Bible and pray about your re-launch plan.*

- *Find two or more other people that will form your Accountability Crew.*
  These can be close friends, other women in your church or mums that you know from your children's school. You can decide to have online or face-to-face meetings. It is important that they read the book so that you are both singing from the same page and can come up with an effective action plan of what you need to do individually and as a team.

- *Do ensure that your action plans are S-M-A-R-T.*
  For this to work, you need to ensure that your actions are **s**pecific, **m**easurable, **a**ttainable, **r**ealistic and within a particular **t**ime-frame. So, for example, a general action could be 'Apply for jobs' but a smart action plan would say 'Apply for two accountancy roles by 24/06/2014'.

- *Be a completer/finisher.*
  Try not to allow your actions to pile up, and do not jump to another action without completing the previous one. Do remember to tick the boxes provided after completing each action.

Action Plan

Enter your relaunch plan for each week in the boxes below.

WEEK 1	Tick when completed. ☐
WEEK 2	Tick when completed. ☐
WEEK 3	Tick when completed. ☐
WEEK 4	Tick when completed. ☐
WEEK 5	Tick when completed. ☐

Get up, Create, Break out

WEEK 6	Tick when completed. ☐
WEEK 7	Tick when completed. ☐
WEEK 8	Tick when completed. ☐
WEEK 9	Tick when completed. ☐
WEEK 10	Tick when completed. ☐
WEEK 11	Tick when completed. ☐
WEEK 12	Tick when completed. ☐

A Quick 'How To' Guide for your Re-launch Action Plan

WEEK 13	Tick when completed. ☐

WEEK 14	Tick when completed. ☐

WEEK 15	Tick when completed. ☐

WEEK 16	Tick when completed. ☐

WEEK 17	Tick when completed. ☐

WEEK 18	Tick when completed. ☐

WEEK 19	Tick when completed. ☐

WEEK 20	Tick when completed.	☐

WEEK 21	Tick when completed.	☐

WEEK 22	Tick when completed.	☐

WEEK 23	Tick when completed.	☐

WEEK 24	Tick when completed.	☐

WEEK 25	Tick when completed.	☐

WEEK 26	Tick when completed.	☐

| WEEK 27 | Tick when completed. | ☐ |

| WEEK 28 | Tick when completed. | ☐ |

| WEEK 29 | Tick when completed. | ☐ |

| WEEK 30 | Tick when completed. | ☐ |

| WEEK 31 | Tick when completed. | ☐ |

| WEEK 32 | Tick when completed. | ☐ |

| WEEK 33+ | Tick when completed. | ☐ |

Epilogue: Still Walking on Water

Bought by Christ
Living for Him
Spirit filled
Desiring radical and supernatural living
Tired of settling for less
Wanting more of God
Walking on water

I wrote this book during a time of great pain and turmoil. I believe God allowed this to be the case so that I can continue to live what I am teaching others to do.

Getting up, creating and breaking out is not always comfortable. In fact it is usually a terrifying experience. In writing this book, I had to get up and stop feeling sorry for myself. I then had to create by articulating my thoughts, knowledge and experience into a manuscript. Finally I had to break out and trust God to take over the publishing and promotion of this book, so it can bless and impact other people. Through it all, God has shown me that it is possible to step out and do the things He has placed in our hearts even when we are faced with all sorts of challenges. I have learnt that God's grace is sufficient and that He is always there even when this doesn't appear to be the case. Beyond all this, His desire is that we shall know Him.

Last year, with tears streaming down my cheeks, I asked God to let me always need Him. Little did I know what I was letting myself in for! God heard my simple prayer, and He has been shaking every area of my life so that I can learn to rely on Him completely. This book is part of my shaking experience. I can no longer live a normal life. I am getting exactly what I asked for, only not in a way that I imagined it would be.

I am currently working on development plans for Smart Opportunities for Women – a UK social enterprise committed to helping skilled women facing disadvantages to re-launch their careers. Its purpose is to respond to a great need which I have seen amongst women within and outside the church. A lot of women are missing-in-action and suffering silently; they are unable to live from a place of purpose and passion because of marriage breakdowns, gender-oppressive cultural backgrounds, unhelpful and imbalanced interpretation of scriptures, and more.

The main areas of activities will include:

- Recycling of clothing items and accessories.
- Providing encouragement and career support.
- Small business development opportunities to enable income-generation and self-sustainability.
- Equipping the church to respond effectively.
- Training church leaders, women group leaders and volunteers.
- Evangelism, discipleship and fellowship through local churches.

Royalties I receive from the sale of this book will go to the work of Smart Opportunities for Women. I am walking on water; pursuing a dream which seems humanly impossible, but with God all things are possible.

I hope this book has blessed you, and I pray that you too will step out and walk on water, knowing fully well that because the Master is beside you, you shall not sink.

Don't hold back; let nothing stop you – only trust God. Let the Word of God guide you as you embark on your re-launch journey.

Useful Websites and Organisations

Advice

ADVICE GUIDE – self-help from citizens' advice.
www.adviceguide.org.uk

ADVISORY, CONCILIATION AND ARBITRATION SERVICE (ACAS) – provides up-to-date information, independent advice and high quality training on employment rights and relations.
www.acas.org,uk

CITIZENS ADVICE BUREAU – helps people resolve their legal, money and other problems by providing free, independent and confidential advice, and by influencing policymakers.
www.citizensadvice.org.uk

DAYCARE TRUST – provides a hotline information service to employers, parents, childcare providers, employers, trade unions, local authorities and policymakers.
www.daycaretrust.org.uk

GINGERBREAD – UK based charity that provides expert advice, practical support and campaign for single parents.
www.gingerbread.org.uk

NATIONAL CAREERS SERVICE – provides information, advice and guidance on learning, training and work opportunities.
www.nationalcareersservice.direct.gov.uk

THE PENSIONS ADVISORY SERVICE – voluntary organisation that provides advice and information about pensions.
www.pensionsadvisoryservice.org.uk

WORKING FAMILIES – a charity that helps working parents achieve work-life balance; its legal helpline provides advice to parents and carers on their employment rights at work.
www.workingfamiles.org.uk

Business

BUSINESS LINK – a helpline providing a quick response service if you have simple questions about starting or running a business. The organization also provides a more in-depth service if you have more complex enquiries.
www.gov.uk/business-support-helpline
www.gov.uk/browse/business/setting-up

EVERYWOMAN – a membership organisation that champions the advancement of women in business.
www.everywoman.com

PROWESS 2.0 – the leading online centre for women in business.
www.prowess.org.uk

Career Re-entry Programs

DAPHNE JACKSON TRUST (U. K. FOUNDATION) – offers two-year flexible, paid, part-time research fellowships at universities or in industry for those on career break from Science, Engineering and Technology careers.
www.daphnejackson.org

INDIE TRAINING FUND – free course for women returners to TV. The course is for women working in TV who have taken a career break for maternity or other reasons, or are about to do so.
www.indietrainingfund.com

L'OREAL AND U.K. RESOURCE CENTER IN SCIENCE, ENGINEERING AND TECHNOLOGY (SET) – offers fellowships for women in science
www.womeninscience.co.uk

Get up, Create, Break out

WELLCOME TRUST – offers a career re-entry fellowship to postdoctoral scientists who have recently decided to recommence a scientific research career after a continuous break of at least two years.
www.wellcome.ac.uk

Career Support

GET UP, CREATE, BREAK OUT – faith-inspired personal and career development resources, events and programmes for women who want to live boldly from a place of purpose and passion.
www.getupcreatebreakout.com

SMART OPPORTUNITIES FOR WOMEN – social enterprise committed to helping skilled women facing disadvantages to re-launch their careers.
www.smartopportunities.org

WOMEN LIKE US – a social enterprise that provides online career advice for women who want to fit work around family, as well as face-to-face support for women on low incomes
www.womenlikeus.org.uk

JOB BOARDS AND RECRUITMENT AGENCIES – flexible part-time jobs

CAPABILITY JANE – a company that helps organisations attract, recruit and on-board professional women returners.
www.capabilityjane.com

CHRISTIAN AU PAIRS – home help childcare provided by Christian girls for Christian families in the UK and beyond.
www.christianaupairs.com

DIVERSITY JOBS – inclusive and diverse careers marketplace.
www.diversityjobs.co.uk

FLEXIBLE WORKS – the home of flexible opportunities.
www.flexible-jobs.co.uk

FLEXOLUTION – creates opportunities for flexible and talented professionals by connecting them to organisations that need them.
www.flexolution.co.uk

MOJOMUMS – recruitment website that helps mums back into work.
www.mojomumsjobs.co.uk

REMOTE EMPLOYMENT – job site for flexible jobs working from home and home business opportunities.
www.remoteemployment.com

TEN 2 TWO – recruitment organisation specialising in flexible and part-time working.
www.ten2two.org

TIMEWISE JOBS – part-time jobs and flexible options for skilled people.
www.timewisejobs.co.uk

WORKING MUMS – job board that connects mums and employers.
www.workingmums.co.uk

Learning and Development

BBC FIRST CLICK – a learning campaign to inspire people to use the Internet.
www.bbc.co.uk/connect/campaigns/first_click.shtml

FREE ENGLISH, MATHS AND LANGUAGE COURSES.
http://mse.me/learnlang

LEARN DIRECT – national helpline providing information and advice on learning, education, training courses and funding.
www.learndirect.co.uk

Get up, Create, Break out

MICROSOFT BIZSPARK – a programme designed to help young technology companies at a time when credit is hard to come by. BizSpark members get direct access to software, developer tools, technical assistance, and server products for three years at no upfront cost. Microsoft also helps promote start-ups with scalable marketing solutions and visibility.
http://www.microsoft.com/BizSpark/

OPENLEARN – you can access free learning materials, study units, quizzes and downloads on the OpenLearn website.
www.open.ac.uk/openlearn

QUICK READS – these exciting, dramatic and funny stories are ideal for adults who've stopped reading or find reading tough, and for regular readers who want a short, fast read. Quick Reads have helped hundreds of thousands of people to pick up books and enjoy reading again.
www.quickreads.org.uk

Money, Saving Tips and Recycling

CONSUMER DIRECT – free online service which advises you about your rights when you buy products and services, and what to do if there's a problem.
www.consumerdirect.gov.uk

ENERGY SAVING TRUST – a non-profit organisation that provides free and impartial advice on how to save energy (insulation, electrical appliances, heating, lighting, etc.)
www.energysavingtrust.org.uk

FREE CYCLE – Free Cycle groups match people who have things they want to get rid of with people who can use them. The goal is to keep usable items out of landfills. Free cycle encourages people to get rid of junk they no longer need and promote community involvement in the process.
www.uk.freecycle.org

MONEY ADVICE SERVICE – an independent service set up by the Government to help people make the most of their money; they give free, unbiased money advice to everyone across the UK – online, over the phone and face to face.
www.moneyadviceservice.org.uk

MONEYMAGPIE – the country's leading site for safe and legitimate money-making opportunities. The site has up-to-date information on ways to earn a bit on the side and a wealth of information on how to help consumers make the most of their money.
www.moneymagpie.com

MONEY SAVING EXPERT – a site dedicated to saving consumers' money on anything and everything by finding the best deals and beating the system. It's based on detailed journalistic research, cutting edge tools and has one of the UK's largest web communities.
www.moneysavingexpert.com

EDUCATION AND STUDY GRANTS
http://mse.me/edugrants

SAYNOTO0870 –lists the equivalent geographical telephone numbers for well-known companies with 0500, 0800, 0808, 0844, 0845, 0870 and 0871 numbers. Save money by looking up alternative numbers.
www.saynoto0870.com

WATER-WISELY (HELPING YOU SAVE WATER) – if you are a Thames Water Supply customer, you can order any of the water-saving devices on this site's page free of charge.
http://www.thameswater-savewatersavemoney.co.uk/products/free-water-saving-pack

Get up, Create, Break out

Volunteering

DO IT
www.do-it.org.uk

VOLUNTEERING ENGLAND
www.volunteering.org.uk

TIME BANK
www.timebank.org.uk

CRIMINAL JUSTICE –helps you find a local criminal justice
organisation where you can volunteer.
www.clinks.org/new-criminal-justice-system

FURTHER EDUCATION INSTITUTIONS – contact the clerk or student
services manager of the College in which you are interested.

HIGHER EDUCATION INSTITUTIONS – to register an interest, contact
the institution through the secretary to the Board of Governors or the
registrar (the title varies depending on the institution).

INDEPENDENT MONITORING BOARDS – every prison establishment
and immigration removal centre throughout England and Wales has
its own Board. Contact the Independent Monitoring Boards
Secretariat for an application pack.
www.imb.gov.uk.

LOCAL COUNCILLORS – for further information about getting elected
as a local councillor, contact the local political party for which you
would want to stand. Your local authority or local library should
have the contact details. Whilst it is possible to be an independent
candidate, the most common route for standing as a councillor is to
be adopted by a local political party.

LONDON COUNCILS / 'BE A COUNCILLOR' CAMPAIGN
www.beacouncillor.org.uk

MAGISTRATES – application forms and information are available from the secretary of the local advisory committee. The name and address can be obtained from the office of the Clerk to the Justices in your local magistrate's court, or from the Office of the Secretary of the Commissions Office.
www.direct.gov.uk/magistrates

PUBLIC APPOINTMENTS – The Public Appointments section of the Cabinet Office website provides details of current vacancies on the boards of UK public bodies and on a range of UK Government committees.
www.publicappointments.cabinetoffice.gov.uk

SCHOOLS – for appointments to governing bodies, apply direct to the school in which you are interested or to your Local Education Authority (LEA). Alternatively, contact the School Governors' One-Stop Shop, which recruits volunteers to become governors in schools across England.
www.sgoss.org.uk

THE POLICE – to become a lay visitor at a police station, or to get involved in the Police Community Consultative Groups, contact your nearest police authority.

OTHER LOCAL GROUPS – use the telephone directory or local library for contact addresses in the local area. Some examples include the Guide Association, YMCA, YWCA, etc. For these you need normally to apply through the national association or regional body, who will put you in touch with the local district commissioner.

Connect

Thanks for being a part of *Get up, Create, Break out*. It is my prayer that as you act on the things which you have read, God will help you access, create and maximise opportunities.

I would love to hear more about how you have used this book. Here are some ways you can keep in touch:

- On the book's website – *www.getupcreatebreakout.com* – you'll find information about our programme and relevant events. This book is the beginning of a powerful network with God at the centre, which is devoted to helping women of all ages re-launch their careers. So do visit the site and stay in touch.

- On Twitter, you can find me at @SmartOpps4Women. Add the hash tag *#getupcreatebreakout* to your tweets about this book and any relevant events.

- On Facebook, like us at:
  www.facebook.com/smartopportunitiesforwomen

- For speaking invitations, or to run an in-house *Get up, Create, Break out* programme or set up a *Get up, Create, Break out* group in your church or community, check out our website at *www.getupcreatebreakout.com* or email me directly at *veronica@smartopportunities.co.uk*.

Hope to hear from you soon!

God's richest blessings,
Veronica